SONGS

OF

FREEDOM:

TALES FROM

THE

REVOLUTION

BCID: 083-7051047
http://www.BookCrossing.com/083-7051047

ISBN: 1441402594

EAN-13: 9781441402592

SONGS OF FREEDOM: TALES FROM THE REVOLUTION

by: Darryl W. Perry, Adam Kokesh, Allison Gibbs, Bonita Honhorst,
Brandon Trent, Danielle Kays, Emma Goldman, Gary Chartier, Gary Franchi,
Henry David Thoreau, James Russell Lowell, Jessica Pacholski, Jim Davidson,
Kimberly Johnson, Melissa Hill, Melody L. (Lewis) Key, Patrick Henry,
Richard Henry Lee, Terri Kurowski, Thomas E. Woods, Jr. & Voltairine de Cleyre

DEDICATION:

To Ron Paul, because you have brought us together to
strengthen the Freedom Movement, without you
the R(EVOL)ution wouldn't exist.

To Adam Kokesh, a true American Patriot and hero,
thank you for speaking the truth.

To Gary Franchi thank you for continuing the work
started by Aaron Russo to Restore the Republic.

To Aaron Russo, you will be missed, thank you for
your work Freedom to Fascism that has opened
the eyes of many Americans,

To Allison Gibbs, Bonita Honhorst, Brandon Trent,
Danielle Kays, Gary Chartier, Jessica Pacholski,
Jim Davidson, Kimberly Johnson, Melissa Hill,
Melody Key,Terri Kurowski & Tom Woods –
thank you for contributing to this work, it
wouldn't exist without you.

To everyone else in the Freedom Movement, past,
present and future – this book is for you!

Table Of Contents

"TRUTH IS TREASON
IN AN EMPIRE OF LIES"

PREFACE

by: Darryl W. Perry

I got the idea for this book about a 6 weeks after the Presidential election of 2008. I began to reflect on the previous 18 months with all of the rallies and events that I (and thousands others) had attended in support of smaller government and more personal freedom. I was reminded that Dr. Paul had become the unofficial spokesman for liberty for this generation. I, and others, see the "rEVOLution" as an extension of the American Revolution started by our ancestors over 230 years ago. While we aren't fighting the British crown for independence; we are fighting an oppressive government for our freedom. We're fighting to protect our Constitutional rights, which have slowly eroded away over the last century.

While this book is inspired by Dr. Paul and in a way dedicated to him; this book is also about more than one man. To borrow a quote from Adam Kokesh, "The freedom movement is bigger than any one party, and any one leader. The revolution of which I speak is a revolution of values, of political culture, and of the understanding of the responsibility of being a good citizen. When that happens, it will be reflected in our political system one way or another, be it through the Republicans, Democrats, Green Party, Constitution Party, or an independent candidate...More than the party or any one candidate, I am committed to this movement, my country, and my principles."

This is a book written by and for everyone in the freedom movement.

*"IT IS DANGEROUS
TO BE RIGHT
WHEN THE GOVERNMENT
IS WRONG."*

VOLTAIRE

Give Me Liberty Speech
March 23, 1775
by: Patrick Henry

No man thinks more highly than I do of the patriotism, as well as
abilities, of the very worthy gentlemen who have just addressed the
House. But different men often see the same subject in different lights;
and, therefore, I hope it will not be thought disrespectful to those
gentlemen if, entertaining as I do opinions of a character very opposite to
theirs, I shall speak forth my sentiments freely and without reserve. This
is no time for ceremony. The question before the House is one of awful
moment to this country. For my own part, I consider it as nothing less than
a question of freedom or slavery; and in proportion to the magnitude of the
subject ought to be the freedom of the debate. It is only in this way that
we can hope to arrive at truth, and fulfill the great responsibility which we
hold to God and our country. Should I keep back my opinions at such a
time, through fear of giving offense, I should consider myself as guilty of
treason towards my country, and of an act of disloyalty toward the Majesty
of Heaven, which I revere above all earthly kings.

Mr. President, it is natural to man to indulge in the illusions of hope. We
are apt to shut our eyes against a painful truth, and listen to the song of
that siren till she transforms us into beasts. Is this the part of wise men,
engaged in a great and arduous struggle for liberty? Are we disposed to be
of the number of those who, having eyes, see not, and, having ears, hear
not, the things which so nearly concern their temporal salvation? For my
part, whatever anguish of spirit it may cost, I am willing to know the
whole truth; to know the worst, and to provide for it.

I have but one lamp by which my feet are guided, and that is the lamp of
experience. I know of no way of judging of the future but by the past. And
judging by the past, I wish to know what there has been in the conduct of
the British ministry for the last ten years to justify those hopes with which
gentlemen have been pleased to solace themselves and the House. Is it that
insidious smile with which our petition has been lately received? Trust it
not, sir; it will prove a snare to your feet. Suffer not yourselves to be
betrayed with a kiss. Ask yourselves how this gracious reception of our

petition comports with those warlike preparations which cover our waters and darken our land. Are fleets and armies necessary to a work of love and reconciliation? Have we shown ourselves so unwilling to be reconciled that force must be called in to win back our love? Let us not deceive ourselves, sir. These are the implements of war and subjugation; the last arguments to which kings resort. I ask gentlemen, sir, what means this martial array, if its purpose be not to force us to submission? Can gentlemen assign any other possible motive for it? Has Great Britain any enemy, in this quarter of the world, to call for all this accumulation of navies and armies? No, sir, she has none. They are meant for us: they can be meant for no other. They are sent over to bind and rivet upon us those chains which the British ministry have been so long forging. And what have we to oppose to them? Shall we try argument? Sir, we have been trying that for the last ten years. Have we anything new to offer upon the subject? Nothing. We have held the subject up in every light of which it is capable; but it has been all in vain. Shall we resort to entreaty and humble supplication? What terms shall we find which have not been already exhausted? Let us not, I beseech you, sir, deceive ourselves. Sir, we have done everything that could be done to avert the storm which is now coming on. We have petitioned; we have remonstrated; we have supplicated; we have prostrated ourselves before the throne, and have implored its interposition to arrest the tyrannical hands of the ministry and Parliament. Our petitions have been slighted; our remonstrances have produced additional violence and insult; our supplications have been disregarded; and we have been spurned, with contempt, from the foot of the throne! In vain, after these things, may we indulge the fond hope of peace and reconciliation. There is no longer any room for hope. If we wish to be free-- if we mean to preserve inviolate those inestimable privileges for which we have been so long contending--if we mean not basely to abandon the noble struggle in which we have been so long engaged, and which we have pledged ourselves never to abandon until the glorious object of our contest shall be obtained--we must fight! I repeat it, sir, we must fight! An appeal to arms and to the God of hosts is all that is left us!

They tell us, sir, that we are weak; unable to cope with so formidable an adversary. But when shall we be stronger? Will it be the next week, or the next year? Will it be when we are totally disarmed, and when a British guard shall be stationed in every house? Shall we gather strength by irresolution and inaction? Shall we acquire the means of effectual resistance by lying supinely on our backs and hugging the delusive phantom of hope, until our enemies shall have bound us hand and foot? Sir, we are not weak if we make a proper use of those means which the God of nature hath placed in our power.

The millions of people, armed in the holy cause of liberty, and in such a country as that which we possess, are invincible by any force which our enemy can send against us. Besides, sir, we shall not fight our battles alone. There is a just God who presides over the destinies of nations, and who will raise up friends to fight our battles for us. The battle, sir, is not to the strong alone; it is to the vigilant, the active, the brave. Besides, sir, we have no election. If we were base enough to desire it, it is now too late to retire from the contest. There is no retreat but in submission and slavery! Our chains are forged! Their clanking may be heard on the plains of Boston! The war is inevitable--and let it come! I repeat it, sir, let it come.

It is in vain, sir, to extenuate the matter. Gentlemen may cry, Peace, Peace-- but there is no peace. The war is actually begun! The next gale that sweeps from the north will bring to our ears the clash of resounding arms! Our brethren are already in the field! Why stand we here idle? What is it that gentlemen wish? What would they have? Is life so dear, or peace so sweet, as to be purchased at the price of chains and slavery? Forbid it, Almighty God! **I know not what course others may take; but as for me, give me liberty or give me death!**

"THE HUMAN RACE DIVIDES ITSELF POLITICALLY
INTO THOSE WHO WANT TO BE CONTROLLED,
AND THOSE WHO HAVE NO SUCH DESIRE."

ROBERT A. HEINLEIN

Dr. Paul Cured my Blindness

March 12, 2008

by: Danielle Kays

If you wear corrective lenses, do you remember how you felt the first time you put on glasses or contacts and could suddenly see things you never even knew you were missing? I remember getting dizzy and even somewhat nauseous because of my new-found ability to see individual leaves on trees and individual pebbles in pavement.

As early voting was about to begin here in Texas, I was still struggling with a decision between McCain and Huckabee. You see, my vision had not yet been corrected, and I was only seeing what the media and the GOP insiders wanted me to see. I had done research on all of the candidates over the last six months or so, but never even bothered to look up Ron Paul because I was convinced he was a fringe candidate who more closely resembled the liberal democrats.

Out of sheer desperation at the thought of having to choose McCain or Huckabee, I finally googled the other remaining candidates. I visited Hillary's website and Obama's, too, looking for any redeeming qualities that would make me feel good about voting for them. As expected, though, they are both WAY too liberal - to the point of being outright Socialists. Then I googled Ron Paul. I'd been fairly observant when the candidates dropped out one by one, and I didn't remember him quitting yet. So I thought, what the heck!

Within the span of a couple of hours spent watching various youtube videos, I began to get that dizzy feeling as my vision began to get clearer. The nausea began to sweep over me as I realized more and more how I d been duped by those who call themselves unbiased journalists as well as other conservative voices, which I had previously thought were correct in their analyses of all things political.

More on Ron Paul later, but Naked Liberty is about much more than one man. He just happens to be the one who got me (and countless others) to finally be able to really think outside the box. When we are able to make that paradigm shift and start looking at EVERYTHING from a new point of view, many say that we have been awakened , and I use that term frequently now.

It s as if I stumbled upon a pair of truth glasses that have allowed me to see past the media s lies, omissions, and not-so-subtle innuendos. These glasses are a permanent correction of my vision, which spurs me to seek information in a relentless pursuit of the truth about our country, our government, our monetary system, our history, our people, and our liberty.

(Painting by Bonita Honhorst)

"AMERICA WAS BORN OF PROTEST,
REVOLUTION, AND MISTRUST OF GOVERNMENT.
SUBSERVIENT SOCIETIES NEITHER MAINTAIN
NOR DESERVE FREEDOM FOR LONG."

RON PAUL

"MEN OF IDEAS VANISH
WHEN FREEDOM VANISHES."

CARL SANDBURG

An Unlikely Education

by: Terri Kurowski

I owe Ron Paul an immeasurable debt of gratitude. As a mother of 3 children, I constantly worry about what goes inside my childrens' minds and bodies. I have some control over what they eat but not as much over what they hear and what is taught to them by others, especially in school. A cursory glance at any history or civics textbook is enough to know that they certainly aren't being taught about the Rule of Law and the foundations upon which our great country was formed. And I often fretted about how I could properly teach my children these principles. That is, until Ron Paul ran for president. Here's my story:

If someone had taken out a crystal ball even as recently as 5 years ago, and showed me my life as it is today, I would have not only laughed hysterically, but also told them that most certainly it was not my life being foretold. Life is like that and the older I get, the more awesome it becomes how seemingly insignificant events and minor happenstance becomes a significant life changing journey.

It really was a dark and stormy night that likely was the seed for what was to come. In August of 1998, shortly after I'd left a job of nearly 20 years, Hurricane Bonnie came to town. Power was out for days and the only news source I could find was a local AM radio station. The morning talk show host, Tony Macrini was quite entertaining as well as being informative regarding the weather conditions and the fallout from the storm. I began listening to him, and sometimes, to the other talk shows that followed.

Life returned to normal, but I still periodically listened to Tony and increasingly found myself either agreeing with him or saying to myself, "hmmm"--he challenged me to think.

Let me back up a bit. I never was particularly interested in politics, even though my parents made my siblings and me register to vote as soon as we turned 18, and we grew up in a household that occasionally discussed politics and political issues. As a child, what little TV I was allowed to watch consisted of news or sports, little else. My parents always read the paper and I suppose I absorbed some information by osmosis.

I'm almost ashamed to admit it but in high school, I was more interested in cheer leading, band and the cutest boy in the class rather than history or civics. In college, I focused on my career path and avoided as many of those types of classes as I possibly could. Sure, I'd read the Constitution and Declaration of Independence, even saw them in person at the National Archives, and I managed to cough up enough information to pass my classes, but little more.

But that doesn't mean that I didn't have a sense of patriotism and justice or that didn't know that this country was the Beacon of Liberty for the world. I'd always considered myself to be lucky to have been born in the US of A. I suppose that came from listening to my grandparents, two of whom immigrated to this country with little more than the shirts on their backs, who talked about such things and how grateful they were for living in a Free land.

Back to Tony. After a while, I became literally addicted to Tony's show. He talked about things such as the Constitution and how it was being abused and what the function of the federal government is. He talked about hotly debated issues such as racism and the War on (Some) Drugs, and discussed them in ways I'd never heard before. He talked about Liberty and the hard-fought and bloody wars that preserved Liberty. A local expert on the War of Northern Aggression, I heard about history in a way that had me riveted to the radio.

One fateful day, Tony said, "get yourself a copy of the Constitution and read if for yourself". So that day, I ordered a copy of the Constitution from the CATO institute (for a mere $1.00) and carry it still today. I read it, and I was astounded with its elegant simplicity and the foresight of the Framers. How had we gone so far off the reservation? Why weren't We the People taught the Constitution itself in school? How did we get a massive, bloated, overbearing federal government when the intent was to protect Life, Liberty and Property?

Shortly thereafter, Tony read a piece by a certain Texas congressman whom I'd never heard of. I don't recall the piece, but I definitely recall saying aloud, "this guy makes sense!!", a phrase I've often heard since, when people read and hear the words of Ron Paul. I looked him up immediately, and became an instant fan.

Thus began my personal Campaign for Liberty and my personal efforts to tell the world about Ron Paul. I won't bore you with every detail of my political journey, but suffice it to say, just as the smoker who quits and becomes an anti-smoking crusader, I became downright evangelical about Liberty, and about Ron Paul. My friends and family often thought I was downright nutty!

Fast forward to 2007, and once again, on the radio, I heard that there was a meetup group meeting in Virginia Beach in support of Ron Paul's candidacy for president. Of course, I went.

It was a rather smallish group, maybe 20 people, but I was fascinated by the attendees. They ranged in age from teens to middle aged, and their backgrounds were very diverse. I was most thrilled of all to meet, in person, an actual middle aged woman who was on the same wavelength as I. This gal and I became fast friends and maintain a very close friendship, bordering sisterhood to this day. During the campaign, she and I were invited to be on Tony's show twice to talk about Ron Paul and Tony dubbed us "The Ronettes"

There were many highlights to the campaign; meeting all the new lovers of Liberty, from every walk of life, that I never knew existed, watching home-made youtubes until the wee hours, the money bombs, the sign-making parties, standing on street corners with signs and receiving many honks and thumbs up, reading the tear-invoking letters from foreigners begging us to help Ron Paul save our country and indeed the world, the very busy booth our group put together for a local Talkfest, and getting to do some friendly "harassment" of Sean Hannity and Glenn Beck in person, our tables at the gun shows, winning the presidential straw poll at the Virginia Republican Advance, and seeing the cross-section of America that drove many miles to show up to vote; the list is endless.

But for me, the biggest highlight of all--and this is where the huge debt of gratitude comes in--was the education my children received simply by being around me and my Liberty loving friends and our continual discussions about Liberty and the Constitution. It is an education that I could neither buy nor could I have ever taught, no matter how fancy the materials, no matter how much time I devoted to it. They must have caught on to the excitement in my voice or perhaps the logical discussions I'd frequently have with others.

I didn't realize just how much they had caught on until they started asking questions--things that normally don't come out of self-absorbed teenage girls or a young boy. My kids started coming home from school and telling me that they'd argued with a classmate or teacher about something that was mentioned in class and they'd ask me for further clarification. So the subject of the discussion over our evening meals often became--and still are-- something regarding the Bill of Rights, private property, self-ownership, the War on (Some) Drugs, the war and so on. As I've learned, so have they. The subject of money and how it works has now been added to the mix. Ron Paul inadvertently gave me credibility to teach my kids.

Even further, my children witnessed their mother, as well as Ron Paul, standing up for what is right in the face of much opposition and scorn. And we held our heads high. I now witness my own children having the courage to do the same whether it's in the face of peer pressure, standing up for a classmate who is being bullied or to a teacher who adores communism.

I could just burst with pride to hear my 11-year old son explain private property or, his favorite, the 2nd Amendment; my 16-year old daughter tell me about how her textbook is ridiculous because its two sentences on the Great Depression were little more than a smear on capitalism, or my 15-year old daughter, the one who is the most into it, write a paper on the ills of the Patriot Act. At this point, my 15-year old plans to major in Economics in college and run for president one day. Even if she doesn't, I'm quite sure none of this would have happened were it not for the Ron Paul r3VOLution. Like Ernie Hancock says, "it's a revolution between the ears" and thanks to Ron Paul, there are three more r3VOLutionaries that Big Government will have to contend with in the very near future.

"WHO THEN IS FREE?
THE WISE MAN WHO
CAN COMMAND HIMSELF."

HORACE

"ALL THAT IS NECESSARY FOR EVIL TO TRIUMPH,
IS FOR GOOD MEN TO DO NOTHING."

EDMUND BURKE

Take the Red Pill

by Thomas E. Woods, Jr.

May 12, 2008

In The Revolution: A Manifesto, Ron Paul says he doesn t believe the claim that most people are indifferent about freedom as long as they re kept entertained and well fed. It s more a lack of knowledge, he says, that keeps people from embracing the free society.

I ve gone back and forth on this, and I m inclined to think the truth is somewhere in between. But I think the cynics, who hold out no hope for the American people at all, are surely wrong.

Case in point:

This nurse had accidentally left her copy of The Revolution: A Manifesto at her nurses station overnight. When she arrived the next morning, fearing the book might be lost, she found to her amazement that the overnight nurse had actually read the entire thing. Not only that, but she had become an instant convert, wanting to spread Ron Paul s message to her friends and family, and get extra copies of his book.

This is a person who, just a day earlier, had supported Hillary Clinton on the grounds that she wanted to see a woman in the White House.

Another person in the same discussion thread says that his own father, once a staunch McCain supporter, is now firmly for Ron Paul and withdrawal from Iraq. Having had a chance to read Dr. Paul s positions for himself, he is now convinced that if all Americans could do so, Ron Paul would be president.

And then there s my own experience. I ll be frank: like most people, I wasn t intellectually creative enough to break free of the phony choices our political system gives us. All I knew for sure was that I wasn t a leftist. Therefore, I lazily concluded, I must be in Rush Limbaugh s camp.

Yes, I was once a full-fledged neoconservative, pretty much from the moment I became politically aware until around 1993.

What jolted me out of it? Among other things, I attended Mises University 1993, put on by the Ludwig von Mises Institute, while a junior at Harvard. It was far and away the most intellectually exciting experience of my college career. (Now I m on the other side of things, actually lecturing at the Mises University program, and almost envious of the students who are about to be introduced to the intellectual pleasures of the Austrian School for the first time.)

Then there s my experience teaching American history and Western civilization to students in New York. I didn t propagandize them, since that isn t appropriate in a college history classroom, but the brighter ones perceived soon enough the chasm separating the late-eighteenth-century America I was describing and the America of today.

From time to time they demanded to know my views on this or that subject, or my political philosophy in general. My protests that I did not want to politicize the classroom or intimidate students who had views different from my own were brushed aside: we just want to know what you think, man!

Lo and behold, it made sense to them. And they d never heard it before. I found myself making converts without really trying. (And no, they weren t just saying so in order to ingratiate themselves into the professor s favor; most of these testimonies came in the form of emails well after the semester had ended.)

All these experiences, I suspect, are not really so unusual.

Set aside those who (à la The Matrix) prefer the blue pill and ignorance over the red pill and knowledge. The fact is, plenty of people want that red pill, even if they don t know it yet   as I myself did not, some 15 years ago now.

That pill can take many forms. I can think of three right away: LewRockwell.com, the Ludwig von Mises Institute, and Ron Paul s new book.

But these things can do the work they are intended to do only if we bring them to people s attention   friends, family, co-workers, whatever.

You know what to do next.

*"FREEDOM IS THE RIGHT
TO ONE'S DIGNITY AS A MAN."*

ARCHIBALD MACLEISH

"MANKIND IS AT ITS BEST
WHEN IT IS MOST FREE."

DANTE ALIGHIERI

Speech from the rEVOLution March

July 12, 2008
by: Adam Kokesh

When I joined the Marines at a little strip mall in Santa Fe, and when I was in boot camp in San Diego, and when I was dodging mortars in Fallujah, I could not have imagined that I would one day share a stage with such renowned speakers. However, to march shoulder to shoulder, and to stand in solidarity with you, is a far greater honor.

It has been said that when in the course of human events, an oppression so revolts its subjects, it becomes necessary to alter or abolish the means of that tyranny. Is it that time when our Bill of Rights is defiled every day? When our adventures abroad threaten our security at home? When the Federal Reserve keeps our free nation enslaved by debt? When the people of the world tremble under the thumb of corporate imperialism? And now our nation is drifting dangerously from freedom to fascism. So I have to ask, is it time? The time is now, the threat is clear, the bands of tyranny are tightening around America, and it is our duty to resist!

As empowered patriots, let us take stock of our commitment to the ideals upon which this country is founded. America without her freedoms is like a body without a soul. The challenge before the Freedom Movement is no less, than to bring about a revolution of values, inspire a renaissance of American politics, and breathe new life into the tortured body of our nation. We will meet that challenge with courage and love, and as always, we the people, will prevail!

To rally the troops of the Revolutionary Army in the winter of 1776, Thomas Paine said, "These are the times that try men's souls. The summer soldier and the sunshine patriot, will in this crisis, shrink from the service of their country; but he that stands by it now, deserves the love and thanks of man and woman. Tyranny, like hell, is not easily conquered."

As Iraq Veterans Against the War, we are resisting an occupation that we once risked our lives for. We swore to support and defend the Constitution of the United States of America, but we found out the hard way that the greatest enemies of the Constitution are not to be found in the sands of some far off land, but rather right here at home! We are your new winter soldiers and we are still defending America.

We bring the values, skills, and commitment that make us warriors to the fight before us today. We are working to end the war by strategically withdrawing our material support and inspiring others to do the same. By advocating for veterans, we honor those who served, and empower soldiers to become successful civilians. With Truth In Recruiting, we are inspiring a generation of young Americans to find a better way to serve this country than dying for empire. By supporting those who are actively resisting, we inspire further resistance, and ensure that soldiers still have the right, as is their duty, to disobey illegal orders.

During the siege of Fallujah, a young Lance Corporal was shot through the side of his flak jacket in a firefight to the west of the city. The bullet hit an artery near his spine. My team was called to help get him to the field hospital at Camp Taqadum. He was on a stretcher in the humvee in front of me, and I watched the Corpsman treating the external wound in a frightened, hurried panic, as the dust from the hot road swirled around us. When we got there, I carried him in as he moaned and writhed in pain, barely conscious. He flailed his arm off the stretcher, and as I put it back by his side I told him, "Don't worry. You made it. You're gonna be OK." But he died only minutes later from the internal bleeding.

I have to live with that memory every day, but I have learned from it. I will not tell you that the band-aids applied by Republicans and Democrats will heal us. I will not pretend that everything is just going to be ok while we are bled dry by tyrants. And if it takes the last full measure of devotion, I will not allow the same fate to befall this country!

This young movement, is getting past the external wounds to the greater evils plaguing this nation. We know, that the greatest threat to American security is the current corruption of our government! No politician has ever ended a war. Civil rights were won in this country not by any legislator, but by a movement. I have great hope for America, but not because of an election. No, my hope comes from you!

Our tragic love affair with the state, has led us to put far too much trust in a government that we hoped could improve our lives, but has instead come to run our lives for us. We have become, as a people, like a frightened, battered, beat down victim of an abusive relationship. A servile, unquestioning, obedient people, will always produce tyrants. We must, as a nation, once again, embrace defiance, rebellion, and resistance!

Every day more and more Americans are avoiding unenforceable taxes, leaving government jobs out of disgust, and sending their kids to college instead of combat. But our efforts as a movement must become unified and deliberate to fully withdraw our compliance and support. Be it with your lives, labor, or tax dollars, stop investing in your own oppression! Guard your communities from the police state! Do not waste a single vote, or a single dollar, on the two-party system! Do not be content merely to grumble and to march while they are using fear, force, and violence as weapons of oppression. We must embrace the opportunity to resist civilly while we still can!

We are compelled to be here for many different reasons, and there is strength in our diversity. As within Iraq Veterans Against the War and Veterans For Peace, we do not need to be uniform to be unified. Take a look at the thoughtful, passionate people around you on this field, and throughout this country. Do not leave here without meeting a new brother or sister in the struggle. Take with you the inspiration to share your passion with someone who does not know they are yet part of our movement. Seek out where you can be most effective in the cause of liberty.

Challenge our force fed culture of unquestioning conformity and compliance. Embrace a world that is not defined by the politics of fear, our obedience producing schools, or the false prophets of the corporate media. As we have been awakened, we must stir the sleeping masses. As the forces of oppression are diligent, so must we toil. As they are committed, we must surpass them. As they step up their efforts, we must rise up to defeat them as a unified movement!

We have been labeled rebels, traitors, enemies of the state. All terms King George would have used to vilify our founders. I, for one, will always rebel against oppression, a traitor only to tyranny, and I would be remiss to not be the enemy of a state, that so blatantly tramples our freedoms.

American values have been nearly vanquished by consumerism, militarism, and authoritarianism. Yellow ribbons and lapel pins will not save this country. When injustice becomes law, resistance becomes duty. The utmost manifestation of love and devotion to America, is today as it always has been, resistance of tyranny! Resist we must, and resist we will!

We will not be silent! We will not obey! We will not let our government destroy our humanity! We will not wait another moment in fear to stand up for what we know to be right! It is time the government starts fearing the people again! It is time that we meet oppression with resistance!

They cannot stop us! Humanity marches on. You can fight it, or fight for it. When we say revolution, we say it with love. As we march onward from this place where we have pledged to each other our lives, our fortunes, and our sacred honor, let us embrace the struggle, cherish the fight, and live in that love. The passion of our hearts will be raised with our fists!

"THE TREE OF LIBERTY MUST BE REFRESHED

FROM TIME TO TIME WITH

THE BLOOD OF PATRIOTS AND TYRANTS."

THOMAS JEFFERSON

"WHEN WE LOSE THE RIGHT
TO BE DIFFERENT,
WE LOSE THE PRIVILEGE TO BE FREE."

CHARLES EVAN HUGHES

Anthem for the Ama-Gi

by: Jim Davidson

When I was young, on a course I did steer
To change all the world with no sense of fear.
To help solve problems that all people face,
I invested my skills for the fate of the race.

Working with friends and working alone,
Learning new facts that had to be known,
Trying new methods, daring to dream
The work was quite endless, or so it did seem.

Failures and victories came by the score;
Whatever I did to open the door
Others would challenge until it was late.
Will the bet pay off? What is our fate?

Who can say what the future may bring,
Will it cause us to weep or cause us to sing?
I don't believe in predestined fate,
The future will be what we choose to create.

Each of us working and earning his property;
Keeping it private with total autonomy.
Having such love for each of these folk
Who yearn to live free and shed the yoke

Of oppression that binds with coercion and fear.
Holding a gun or arrow or spear,
Taking up arms for defense of our selves so
No one is master or owner or slave, no

Nobody owns you or me or another.
Nobody plays our father or mother.
We live together or we live far apart
Each choosing his path be it silly or smart.

We are the tribe of freedom you see.

In cuneiform writing they say "Ama-Gi"
The most ancient way of writing we're free,
In wedges of clay before 2000 BC.

For four thousand years now people have known
That freedom is greatest when each is left alone.
No central planners, no central plan
Can make as much difference as one single man

Or woman or child, it matters not which:
The individual holds the key, turns the switch,
Unlocks the door to the future we seek
Next century, next year, or even next week.

Destiny is what we choose to create,
It never has been a matter of fate.
We are not robots to follow in line,
Shuffling along without reason or sign.

I am just me, this guy that you know,
You are just you with your knowledge in tow.
No numbers, no license, no permissions, no crime,
Autonomous factors with reason and rhyme.

True there are those who can't or won't see
That initiating force is wrong as can be.
They act in great haste, they do such a wrong,
We must protect the rest who belong,

Not to each other but each to herself and
Coercing none to gain wealth or land.
The things that we want come best in exchange
For things that we have or produce in a range

Of quality and value that each of us can
Make or devise by some personal plan.
Respecting you while you respect me
Guiding each other and others to see

That all of the future is unwritten as yet
And if we work smart we may still win that bet.

Laying the base on foundation of rock
So that battered by time it will take every shock.

From bottom to top, we build to the stars,
Knowing that what awaits us on Mars
Is another world of possibility, and more
Beyond Mars to a far galaxy's shore.

We travel through space, we travel through time.
There is no mountain that we cannot climb.
We face the future both together and apart,
A journey of miles with but one step to start.

The best thing is taking each seriously.
Respecting the fact of the autonomy
Of each person in order to give them the space
To develop and grow just at their own pace.

We are the Tribe of the Free: Ama-Gi,
Whatever we do, we always live free.

"NEVER TRUST YOUR GOVERNMENT.
THE PRICE OF FREEDOM IS ETERNAL VIGILANCE.
A REVOLUTION IS NEEDED EVERY TWENTY YEARS
JUST TO KEEP THE GOVERNMENT HONEST."

THOMAS JEFFERSON

Sine Wave

by: Gary Chartier

The eye in the sky stares down from on high
    at the thralls who toil below,
while the mushroom cloud, like a billowing shroud,
    lights up the earth with its glow.
The land is dead, and the blood runs red
    of the ones who ve died to be free,
and the tyrant s laugh turns our hopes to chaff
    as death blows in from the sea.
The songs in the air are the cries of despair
    of a people whose home is Hell,
whose ears are filled with the screams of the killed
    and the toll of the final bell.
With a future bright nowhere in sight
    and death coming up with the sun,
we watch and wait, in terror great,
    til our course at last is run.
Yet we know in our hearts   it comes with a start,
    as bursts through the dark a ray
that the tyrants must fall when rebels call
    at the dawn of a fair, new day.
Then the deed is done, the victory won:
    the blood-sown seed bears fruit,
for the ivory tower, the symbol of power,
    is plucked up both branch and root.
But there s somewhat amiss: no signs of bliss
    have filled our land anew,
for the ones who arose, and the tyrants opposed
    were all-too-human, too.
So the eye in the sky *still* stares from on high
    at us, thralls who toil below.
Our hope has died, and so still we cry
    for the sight of freedom s glow.

"OPEN YOUR EYES.
ACCEPT THE PAINFUL TRUTH.
DO SOMETHING TO CORRECT THE WRONG."

THOMAS PAINE

FREEDOM

by: Darryl W. Perry

Freedom

Rings

Eternally

Everywhere

Demanding

Only your

Mind

"YOUR HEART IS FREE;
HAVE THE COURAGE TO FOLLOW IT!"

MALCOM WALLACE

Wake-up, and Grasp Your Freedom

August 5, 1999
by: Gary Franchi

Pull the wool over your eyes
Ye people of today
Continue to believe the media's lies
In the glory of yesterday
The wars we ve won and lost
Have all been just a game
All at the taxpayers cost
And the politician s fame
Soon the "blue berets" will come
To take our guns away
They ll pull the countries all to one
Then blue flags will wave
The Constitution will be scraped
Our people will be caged
True Americans won t stand for this
We ll fight till we don t bleed
Our fore fathers sure hadn't planed for this
United Nations greed
We ll stop them   fore they hit the sea
When it s over, this country will be free.

"ONLY A VIRTUOUS PEOPLE ARE CAPABLE OF FREEDOM.
AS NATIONS BECOME CORRUPT AND VICIOUS,
THEY HAVE MORE NEED OF MASTERS."

BENJAMIN FRANKLIN

My Pledge

November 27, 2000

by: Gary Franchi

Standing on
the oceans edge,
To the flag I take
The pledge,
Of allegiance to
My country lies,
Not just where
The eagle flies,
But to the people,
Of this land,
If everyone would
Raise their hand,
Open their eyes and
Take a stand,
Circular lies and
Congressional committees,
The citizens should
Leave the cities,
To one place,
The peoples find,
To restore this
Country s piece of mind.

"GIVE ME LIBERTY OR GIVE ME DEATH"

PATRICK HENRY

FREEDOM
INDEPENDENT NOW AND FOREVER
PEACE
LOVE
LIBERTY
NOLI ME TANGERE

*"...ALL MEN ARE CREATED EQUAL,
THAT THEY ARE ENDOWED
BY THEIR CREATOR WITH
CERTAIN UNALIENABLE RIGHTS,
THAT AMONG THESE ARE
LIFE, LIBERTY, AND
THE PURSUIT OF HAPPINESS."*

DECLERATION OF INDEPENCE

The Bell Will Never Ring

by: Melissa Hill

Kept secure in the crowded cell
Surrounded by illusionary walls
Waiting endlessly for the bell
To release us into dreamt of halls&

Hearing a distant chime ring
Sadly not the bell s mark
Close enough to make some sing
Yet not the match to set a spark

Circling around in a wave
We only reach a bottomless pit
Feebly grasping, trying to save
What s left of liberty while we sit

Ten years suddenly pass by
Walls are taller with no end
Quietly listening and wondering why
Our own hearing is what we bend!

"IF A NATION EXPECTS
TO BE IGNORANT AND FREE,
IN A STATE OF CIVILIZATION,
IT EXPECTS WHAT NEVER WAS
AND NEVER WILL BE."

THOMAS JEFFERSON

Patriotism:
A Menace to Liberty

by: Emma Goldman

WHAT is patriotism? Is it love of one's birthplace, the place of
childhood's recollections and hopes, dreams and aspirations? Is it the place
where, in childlike naivety, we would watch the fleeting clouds, and
wonder why we, too, could not run so swiftly? The place where we would
count the milliard glittering stars, terror-stricken lest each one "an eye
should be," piercing the very depths of our little souls? Is it the place
where we would listen to the music of the birds, and long to have wings to
fly, even as they, to distant lands? Or the place where we would sit at
mother's knee, enraptured by wonderful tales of great deeds and
conquests? In short, is it love for the spot, every inch representing dear and
precious recollections of a happy, joyous, and playful childhood?

If that were patriotism, few American men of today could be called
upon to be patriotic, since the place of play has been turned into factory,
mill, and mine, while deafening sounds of machinery have replaced the
music of the birds. Nor can we longer hear the tales of great deeds, for the
stories our mothers tell today are but those of sorrow, tears, and grief.

What, then, is patriotism? "Patriotism, sir, is the last resort of
scoundrels," said Dr. Johnson. Leo Tolstoy, the greatest anti-patriot of our
times, defines patriotism as the principle that will justify the training of
wholesale murderers; a trade that requires better equipment for the
exercise of man-killing than the making of such necessities of life as
shoes, clothing, and houses; a trade that guarantees better returns and
greater glory than that of the average workingman.

Gustave Hervé, another great anti-patriot, justly calls patriotism a
superstition--one far more injurious, brutal, and inhumane than religion.
The superstition of religion originated in man's inability to explain natural
phenomena. That is, when primitive man heard thunder or saw the
lightning, he could not account for either, and therefore concluded that
back of them must be a force greater than himself. Similarly he saw a
supernatural force in the rain, and in the various other changes in nature.

Patriotism, on the other hand, is a superstition artificially created and maintained through a network of lies and falsehoods; a superstition that robs man of his self-respect and dignity, and increases his arrogance and conceit.

Indeed, conceit, arrogance, and egotism are the essentials of patriotism. Let me illustrate. Patriotism assumes that our globe is divided into little spots, each one surrounded by an iron gate. Those who have had the fortune of being born on some particular spot, consider themselves better, nobler, grander, more intelligent than the living beings inhabiting any other spot. It is, therefore, the duty of everyone living on that chosen spot to fight, kill, and die in the attempt to impose his superiority upon all the others.

The inhabitants of the other spots reason in like manner, of course, with the result that, from early infancy, the mind of the child is poisoned with bloodcurdling stories about the Germans, the French, the Italians, Russians, etc. When the child has reached manhood, he is thoroughly saturated with the belief that he is chosen by the Lord himself to defend his country against the attack or invasion of any foreigner. It is for that purpose that we are clamoring for a greater army and navy, more battleships and ammunition. It is for that purpose that America has within a short time spent four hundred million dollars. Just think of it--four hundred million dollars taken from the produce of the people. For surely it is not the rich who contribute to patriotism. They are cosmopolitans, perfectly at home in every land. We in America know well the truth of this. Are not our rich Americans Frenchmen in France, Germans in Germany, or Englishmen in England? And do they not squandor with cosmopolitan grace fortunes coined by American factory children and cotton slaves? Yes, theirs is the patriotism that will make it possible to send messages of condolence to a despot like the Russian Tsar, when any mishap befalls him, as President Roosevelt did in the name of his people, when Sergius was punished by the Russian revolutionists.

It is a patriotism that will assist the arch-murderer, Diaz, in destroying thousands of lives in Mexico, or that will even aid in arresting Mexican revolutionists on American soil and keep them incarcerated in American prisons, without the slightest cause or reason.

But, then, patriotism is not for those who represent wealth and power. It is good enough for the people. It reminds one of the historic wisdom of

Frederick the Great, the bosom friend of Voltaire, who said: "Religion is a fraud, but it must be maintained for the masses."

That patriotism is rather a costly institution, no one will doubt after considering the following statistics. The progressive increase of the expenditures for the leading armies and navies of the world during the last quarter of a century is a fact of such gravity as to startle every thoughtful student of economic problems. It may be briefly indicated by dividing the time from 1881 to 1905 into five-year periods, and noting the disbursements of several great nations for army and navy purposes during the first and last of those periods. From the first to the last of the periods noted the expenditures of Great Britain increased from $2,101,848,936 to $4,143,226,885, those of France from $3,324,500,000 to $3,455,109,900, those of Germany from $725,000,200 to $2,700,375,600, those of the United States from $1,275,500,750 to $2,650,900,450, those of Russia from $1,900,975,500 to $5,250,445,100, those of Italy from $1,600,975,750 to $1,755,500,100, and those of Japan from $182,900,500 to $700,925,475.

The military expenditures of each of the nations mentioned increased in each of the five-year periods under review. During the entire interval from 1881 to 1905 Great Britain's outlay for her army increased fourfold, that of the United States was tripled, Russia's was doubled, that of Germany increased 35 per cent., that of France about 15 per cent., and that of Japan nearly 500 per cent. If we compare the expenditures of these nations upon their armies with their total expenditures for all the twenty-five years ending with 1905, the proportion rose as follows:

In Great Britain from 20 per cent. to 37; in the United States from 15 to 23; in France from 16 to 18; in Italy from 12 to 15; in Japan from 12 to 14. On the other hand, it is interesting to note that the proportion in Germany decreased from about 58 per cent. to 25, the decrease being due to the enormous increase in the imperial expenditures for other purposes, the fact being that the army expenditures for the period of 1901-5 were higher than for any five-year period preceding. Statistics show that the countries in which army expenditures are greatest, in proportion to the total national revenues, are Great Britain, the United States, Japan, France, and Italy, in the order named.

The showing as to the cost of great navies is equally impressive. During the twenty-five years ending with 1905 naval expenditures increased approximately as follows: Great Britain, 300 per cent.; France 60 per cent.; Germany 600 per cent.; the United States 525 per cent.; Russia 300 per cent.; Italy 250 per cent.; and Japan, 700 per cent. With the exception of Great Britain, the United States spends more for naval purposes than any other nation, and this expenditure bears also a larger proportion to the entire national disbursements than that of any other power. In the period 1881-5, the expenditure for the United States navy was $6.20 out of each $100 appropriated for all national purposes; the amount rose to $6.60 for the next five-year period, to $8.10 for the next, to $11.70 for the next, and to $16.40 for 1901-5. It is morally certain that the outlay for the current period of five years will show a still further increase.

The rising cost of militarism may be still further illustrated by computing it as a per capita tax on population. From the first to the last of the five-year periods taken as the basis for the comparisons here given, it has risen as follows: In Great Britain, from $18.47 to $52.50; in France, from $19.66 to $23.62; in Germany, from $10.17 to $15.51; in the United States, from $5.62 to $13.64; in Russia, from $6.14 to $8.37; in Italy, from $9.59 to $11.24, and in Japan from 86 cents to $3.11.

It is in connection with this rough estimate of cost per capita that the economic burden of militarism is most appreciable. The irresistible conclusion from available data is that the increase of expenditure for army and navy purposes is rapidly surpassing the growth of population in each of the countries considered in the present calculation. In other words, a continuation of the increased demands of militarism threatens each of those nations with a progressive exhaustion both of men and resources.

The awful waste that patriotism necessitates ought to be sufficient to cure the man of even average intelligence from this disease. Yet patriotism demands still more. The people are urged to be patriotic and for that luxury they pay, not only by supporting their "defenders," but even by sacrificing their own children. Patriotism requires allegiance to the flag, which means obedience and readiness to kill father, mother, brother, sister.

The usual contention is that we need a standing army to protect the country from foreign invasion. Every intelligent man and woman knows, however, that this is a myth maintained to frighten and coerce the foolish. The governments of the world, knowing each other's interests, do not invade each other. They have learned that they can gain much more by international arbitration of disputes than by war and conquest. Indeed, as

Carlyle said, "War is a quarrel between two thieves too cowardly to fight their own battle; therefore they take boys from one village and another village, stick them into uniforms, equip them with guns, and let them loose like wild beasts against each other."

It does not require much wisdom to trace every war back to a similar cause. Let us take our own Spanish-American war, supposedly a great and patriotic event in the history of the United States. How our hearts burned with indignation against the atrocious Spaniards! True, our indignation did not flare up spontaneously. It was nurtured by months of newspaper agitation, and long after Butcher Weyler had killed off many noble Cubans and outraged many Cuban women. Still, in justice to the American Nation be it said, it did grow indignant and was willing to fight, and that it fought bravely. But when the smoke was over, the dead buried, and the cost of the war came back to the people in an increase in the price of commodities and rent--that is, when we sobered up from our patriotic spree it suddenly dawned on us that the cause of the Spanish-American war was the consideration of the price of sugar; or, to be more explicit, that the lives, blood, and money of the American people were used to protect the interests of American capitalists, which were threatened by the Spanish government. That this is not an exaggeration, but is based on absolute facts and figures, is best proven by the attitude of the American government to Cuban labor. When Cuba was firmly in the clutches of the United States, the very soldiers sent to liberate Cuba were ordered to shoot Cuban workingmen during the great cigarmakers' strike, which took place shortly after the war.

Nor do we stand alone in waging war for such causes. The curtain is beginning to be lifted on the motives of the terrible Russo-Japanese war, which cost so much blood and tears. And we see again that back of the fierce Moloch of war stands the still fiercer god of Commercialism. Kuropatkin, the Russian Minister of War during the Russo-Japanese struggle, has revealed the true secret behind the latter. The Tsar and his Grand Dukes, having invested money in Corean concessions, the war was forced for the sole purpose of speedily accumulating large fortunes.

The contention that a standing army and navy is the best security of peace is about as logical as the claim that the most peaceful citizen is he who goes about heavily armed. The experience of every-day life fully proves that the armed individual is invariably anxious to try his strength.

The same is historically true of governments. Really peaceful countries do not waste life and energy in war preparations, With the result that peace is maintained.

However, the clamor for an increased army and navy is not due to any foreign danger. It is owing to the dread of the growing discontent of the masses and of the international spirit among the workers. It is to meet the internal enemy that the Powers of various countries are preparing themselves; an enemy, who, once awakened to consciousness, will prove more dangerous than any foreign invader.

The powers that have for centuries been engaged in enslaving the masses have made a thorough study of their psychology. They know that the people at large are like children whose despair, sorrow, and tears can be turned into joy with a little toy. And the more gorgeously the toy is dressed, the louder the colors, the more it will appeal to the million-headed child.

An army and navy represents the people's toys. To make them more attractive and acceptable, hundreds and thousands of dollars are being spent for the display of these toys. That was the purpose of the American government in equipping a fleet and sending it along the Pacific coast, that every American citizen should be made to feel the pride and glory of the United States. The city of San Francisco spent one hundred thousand dollars for the entertainment of the fleet; Los Angeles, sixty thousand; Seattle and Tacoma, about one hundred thousand. To entertain the fleet, did I say? To dine and wine a few superior officers, while the "brave boys" had to mutiny to get sufficient food. Yes, two hundred and sixty thousand dollars were spent on fireworks, theatre parties, and revelries, at a time when men, women, and child}en through the breadth and length of the country were starving in the streets; when thousands of unemployed were ready to sell their labor at any price.

Two hundred and sixty thousand dollars! What could not have been accomplished with such an enormous sum? But instead of bread and shelter, the children of those cities were taken to see the fleet, that it may remain, as one of the newspapers said, "a lasting memory for the child."

A wonderful thing to remember, is it not? The implements of civilized slaughter. If the mind of the child is to be poisoned with such memories, what hope is there for a true realization of human brotherhood?

We Americans claim to be a peace-loving people. We hate bloodshed;

we are opposed to violence. Yet we go into spasms of joy over the possibility of projecting dynamite bombs from flying machines upon helpless citizens. We are ready to hang, electrocute, or lynch anyone, who, from economic necessity, will risk his own life in the attempt upon that of some industrial magnate. Yet our hearts swell with pride at the thought that America is becoming the most powerful nation on earth, and that it will eventually plant her iron foot on the necks of all other nations.

Such is the logic of patriotism.

Considering the evil results that patriotism is fraught with for the average man, it is as nothing compared with the insult and injury that patriotism heaps upon the soldier himself,--that poor, deluded victim of superstition and ignorance. He, the savior of his country, the protector of his nation,--what has patriotism in store for him? A life of slavish submission, vice, and perversion, during peace; a life of danger, exposure, and death, during war.

While on a recent lecture tour in San Francisco, I visited the Presidio, the most beautiful spot overlooking the Bay and Golden Gate Park. Its purpose should have been playgrounds for children, gardens and music for the recreation of the weary. Instead it is made ugly, dull, and gray by barracks,--barracks wherein the rich would not allow their dogs to dwell. In these miserable shanties soldiers are herded like cattle; here they waste their young days, polishing the boots and brass buttons of their superior officers. Here, too, I saw the distinction of classes: sturdy sons of a free Republic, drawn up in line like convicts, saluting every passing shrimp of a lieutenant. American equality, degrading manhood and elevating the uniform!

Barrack life further tends to develop tendencies of sexual perversion. It is gradually producing along this line results similar to European military conditions. Havelock Ellis, the noted writer on sex psychology, has made a thorough study of the subject. I quote: "Some of the barracks are great centers of male prostitution.... The number of soldiers who prostitute themselves is greater than we are willing to believe. It is no exaggeration to say that in certain regiments the presumption is in favor of the venality of the majority of the men.... On summer evenings Hyde Park and the neighborhood of Albert Gate are full of guardsmen and others plying a lively trade, and with little disguise, in uniform or out.... In most cases the proceeds form a comfortable addition to Tommy Atkins' pocket money."

To what extent this perversion has eaten its way into the army and navy can best be judged from the fact that special houses exist for this form of prostitution. The practice is not limited to England; it is universal. "Soldiers are no less sought after in France than in England or in Germany, and special houses for military prostitution exist both in Paris and the garrison towns."

Had Mr. Havelock Ellis included America in his investigation of sex perversion, he would have found that the same conditions prevail in our army and navy as in those of other countries. The growth of the standing army inevitably adds to the spread of sex perversion; the barracks are the incubators.

Aside from the sexual effects of barrack life, it also tends to unfit the soldier for useful labor after leaving the army. Men, skilled in a trade, seldom enter the army or navy, but even they, after a military experience, find themselves totally unfitted for their former occupations. Having acquired habits of idleness and a taste for excitement and adventure, no peaceful pursuit can content them. Released from the army, they can turn to no useful work. But it is usually the social riff-raff, discharged prisoners and the like, whom either the struggle for life or their own inclination drives into the ranks. These, their military term over, again turn to their former life of crime, more brutalized and degraded than before. It is a well-known fact that in our prisons there is a goodly number of ex-soldiers; while, on the other hand, the army and navy are to a great extent plied with ex-convicts.

Of all the evil results I have just described none seems to me so detrimental to human integrity as the spirit patriotism has produced in the case of Private William Buwalda. Because he foolishly believed that one can be a soldier and exercise his rights as a man at the same time, the military authorities punished him severely. True, he had served his country fifteen years, during which time his record was unimpeachable. According to Gen. Funston, who reduced Buwalda's sentence to three years, "the first duty of an officer or an enlisted man is unquestioned obedience and loyalty to the government, and it makes no difference whether he approves of that government or not." Thus Funston stamps the true character of allegiance. According to him, entrance into the army abrogates the principles of the Declaration of Independence.

What a strange development of patriotism that turns a thinking being into a loyal machine!

In justification of this most outrageous sentence of Buwalda, Gen. Funston tells the American people that the soldier's action was "a serious crime equal to treason." Now, what did this "terrible crime" really consist of? Simply in this: William Buwalda was one of fifteen hundred people who attended a public meeting in San Francisco; and, oh, horrors, he shook hands with the speaker, Emma Goldman. A terrible crime, indeed, which the General calls "a great military offense, infinitely worse than desertion."

Can there be a greater indictment against patriotism than that it will thus brand a man a criminal, throw him into prison, and rob him of the results of fifteen years of faithful service?

Buwalda gave to his country the best years of his life and his very manhood. But all that was as nothing. Patriotism is inexorable and, like all insatiable monsters, demands all or nothing. It does not admit that a soldier is also a human being, who has a right to his own feelings and opinions, his own inclinations and ideas. No, patriotism can not admit of that. That is the lesson which Buwalda was made to learn; made to learn at a rather costly, though not at a useless price. When he returned to freedom, he had lost his position in the army, but he regained his self-respect. After all, that is worth three years of imprisonment.

A writer on the military conditions of America, in a recent article, commented on the power of the military man over the civilian in Germany. He said, among other things, that if our Republic had no other meaning than to guarantee all citizens equal rights, it would have just cause for existence. I am convinced that the writer was not in Colorado during the patriotic régime of General Bell. He probably would have changed his mind had he seen how, in the name of patriotism and the Republic, men were thrown into bull-pens, dragged about, driven across the border, and subjected to all kinds of indignities. Nor is that Colorado incident the only one in the growth of military power in the United States. There is hardly a strike where troops and militia do not come to the rescue of those in power, and where they do not act as arrogantly and brutally as do the men wearing the Kaiser's uniform. Then, too, we have the Dick military law. Had the writer forgotten that?

A great misfortune with most of our writers is that they are absolutely ignorant on current events, or that, lacking honesty, they will not speak of these matters. And so it has come to pass that the Dick military law was rushed through Congress with little discussion and still less publicity,--a law which gives the President the power to turn a peaceful citizen into a bloodthirsty man-killer, supposedly for the defense of the country, in reality for the protection of the interests of that particular party whose mouthpiece the President happens to be.

Our writer claims that militarism can never become such a power in America as abroad, since it is voluntary with us, while compulsory in the Old World. Two very important facts, however, the gentleman forgets to consider. First, that conscription has created in Europe a deep-seated hatred of militarism among all classes of society. Thousands of young recruits enlist under protest and, once in the army, they will use every possible means to desert. Second, that it is the compulsory feature of militarism which has created a tremendous anti-militarist movement, feared by European Powers far more than anything else. After all, the greatest bulwark of capitalism is militarism. The very moment the latter is undermined, capitalism will totter. True, we have no conscription; that is, men are not usually forced to enlist in the army, but we have developed a far more exacting and rigid force--necessity. Is it not a fact that during industrial depressions there is a tremendous increase in the number of enlistments? The trade of militarism may not be either lucrative or honorable, but it is better than tramping the country in search of work, standing in the bread line, or sleeping in municipal lodging houses. After all, it means thirteen dollars per month, three meals a day, and a place to sleep. Yet even necessity is not sufficiently strong a factor to bring into the army an element of character and manhood. No wonder our military authorities complain of the "poor material" enlisting in the army and navy. This admission is a very encouraging sign. It proves that there is still enough of the spirit of independence and love of liberty left in the average American to risk starvation rather than don the uniform.

Thinking men and women the world over are beginning to realize that patriotism is too narrow and limited a conception to meet the necessities of our time. The centralization of power has brought into being an international feeling of solidarity among the oppressed nations of the world; a solidarity which represents a greater harmony of interests between the workingman of America and his brothers abroad than between the American miner and his exploiting compatriot; a solidarity which fears not foreign invasion, because it is bringing all the workers to the point when they will say to their masters, "Go and do your own killing. We have done it long enough for you."

This solidarity is awakening the consciousness of even the soldiers, they, too, being flesh of the flesh of the great human family. A solidarity that has proven infallible more than once during past struggles, and which has been the impetus inducing the Parisian soldiers, during the Commune of 1871, to refuse to obey when ordered to shoot their brothers. It has given courage to the men who mutinied on Russian warships during recent years. It will eventually bring about the uprising of all the oppressed and downtrodden against their international exploiters.

The proletariat of Europe has realized the great force of that solidarity and has, as a result, inaugurated a war against patriotism and its bloody spectre, militarism. Thousands of men fill the prisons of France, Germany, Russia, and the Scandinavian countries, because they dared to defy the ancient superstition. Nor is the movement limited to the working class; it has embraced representatives in all stations of life, its chief exponents being men and women prominent in art, science, and letters.

America will have to follow suit. The spirit of militarism has already permeated all walks of life. Indeed, I am convinced that militarism is growing a greater danger here than anywhere else, because of the many bribes capitalism holds out to those whom it wishes to destroy.

The beginning has already been made in the schools. Evidently the government holds to the Jesuitical conception, "Give me the child mind, and I will mould the man." Children are trained in military tactics, the glory of military achievements extolled in the curriculum, and the youthful minds perverted to suit the government. Further, the youth of the country is appealed to in glaring posters to join the army and navy. "A fine chance to see the world!" cries the governmental huckster. Thus innocent boys are morally shanghaied into patriotism, and the military Moloch strides conquering through the Nation.

The American workingman has suffered so much at the hands of the soldier, State and Federal, that he is quite justified in his disgust with, and his opposition to, the uniformed parasite. However, mere denunciation will not solve this great problem. What we need is a propaganda of education for the soldier: antipatriotic literature that will enlighten him as to the real horrors of his trade, and that will awaken his consciousness to his true relation to the man to whose labor he owes his very existence. It is precisely this that the authorities fear most. It is already high treason for a soldier to attend a radical meeting. No doubt they will also stamp it high treason for a soldier to read a radical pamphlet. But, then, has not authority from time immemorial stamped every step of progress as treasonable? Those, however, who earnestly strive for social reconstruction can well afford to face all that; for it is probably even more important to carry the truth into the barracks than into the factory. When we have undermined the patriotic lie, we shall have cleared the path for that great structure wherein all nationalities shall be united into a universal brotherhood, --a truly FREE SOCIETY.

"WHEN LAW AND MORALITY CONTRADICT EACH
OTHER, THE CITIZEN HAS THE CRUEL ALTERNATIVE
OF EITHER LOSING HIS MORAL SENSE
OR LOSING HIS RESPECT FOR THE LAW."

FREDERIC BASTIAT

"IS FREEDOM ANYTHING ELSE THAN
THE RIGHT TO LIVE AS WE WISH?
NOTHING ELSE."

EPICTETUS

Coercion or Consent

by: Jim Davidson

Recently, I had a discussion about the matter of paying taxes with someone who claims to be libertarian. I pointed out that one of the consequences of demanding compulsory taxes to fund government functions, any government functions, is death.

An example is the seven dozen Texans butchered, gassed, murdered, detonated, and burned to death in their church near Waco, Texas in 1993. The matter for which they were first confronted was about $200 in unpaid taxes on each conceivable count of automatic firearms possession, in the extremely unlikely event that any such weapons were to be found. (Subsequently, a number of semi-auto rifles were reconfigured to fire two rounds on a single trigger pull with the side effect that the second round would always jam. On the basis of this "evidence," some convictions were obtained on firearms charges, I believe.)

A necessary consequence of compulsory taxation is death.

On that side of the discussion is compulsion, coercion, brutality, and force. There are Americans who believe in these things, who insist that they are necessary, and who demand that everyone must obey. Those who are commanded to pay taxes must pay them. If the consequence of their unwillingness to cooperate with their own destruction is death, some are okay with that.

I am not okay with it.

I am defiance. I am for consent, cooperation, and voluntary behavior. I defy the order to obey. I defy the demand for compulsion. I defy the command economy. I am defiance.

There is no agreement between compulsion and consent. There is no reasonable middle ground. There is no possibility of working together. There is either compulsion, coercion, command, and brutality, or there is consent, cooperation, and choice.

I stand for consent. I stand for free choice. That means, necessarily, essentially, and vitally, that I stand against anyone who prefers compulsion, who excuses compulsion, who demands compulsion.

And if that doesn t work for you, if that doesn t build up your party, if that doesn t seem agreeable, if that hurts your feelings, too bad.

You can cavil, equivocate, and compromise all you want with evil. Compulsion is evil. And it isn t going to get better by arguing with it.

"THERE'S NO WAY TO RULE INNOCENT MEN.
THE ONLY POWER GOVERNMENT HAS
IS THE POWER TO CRACK DOWN ON CRIMINALS.
WELL, WHEN THERE AREN'T ENOUGH CRIMINALS,
ONE MAKES THEM.
ONE DECLARES SO MANY THINGS TO BE A CRIME
THAT IT BECOMES IMPOSSIBLE
FOR MEN TO LIVE WITHOUT BREAKING LAWS."

AYN RAND

"A PATRIOT MUST ALWAYS BE READY TO
DEFEND HIS COUNTRY AGAINST HIS GOVERNMENT."

EDWARD ABBEY

On the Duty of Civil Disobedience

[1849, original title: Resistance to Civil government]

by: Henry David Thoreau

I heartily accept the motto, "That government is best which governs least"; and I should like to see it acted up to more rapidly and systematically. Carried out, it finally amounts to this, which also I believe —"That government is best which governs not at all"; and when men are prepared for it, that will be the kind of government which they will have. Government is at best but an expedient; but most governments are usually, and all governments are sometimes, inexpedient. The objections which have been brought against a standing army, and they are many and weighty, and deserve to prevail, may also at last be brought against a standing government. The standing army is only an arm of the standing government. The government itself, which is only the mode which the people have chosen to execute their will, is equally liable to be abused and perverted before the people can act through it. Witness the present Mexican war, the work of comparatively a few individuals using the standing government as their tool; for in the outset, the people would not have consented to this measure.

This American government—what is it but a tradition, though a recent one, endeavoring to transmit itself unimpaired to posterity, but each instant losing some of its integrity? It has not the vitality and force of a single living man; for a single man can bend it to his will. It is a sort of wooden gun to the people themselves. But it is not the less necessary for this; for the people must have some complicated machinery or other, and hear its din, to satisfy that idea of government which they have. Governments show thus how successfully men can be imposed upon, even impose on themselves, for their own advantage. It is excellent, we must all allow. Yet this government never of itself furthered any enterprise, but by the alacrity with which it got out of its way. *It* does not keep the country free. *It* does not settle the West. *It* does not educate. The character inherent in the American people has done all that has been accomplished; and it would have done somewhat more, if the government had not sometimes got in its way. For government is an expedient, by which men would fain succeed in letting one another alone; and, as has been said, when it is most expedient, the governed are most let alone by it. Trade and commerce, if they were not made of india-rubber, would never manage to bounce over obstacles which legislators are continually putting in their way; and if one were to judge these men wholly by the effects of their actions and not partly by their intentions, they would deserve to be classed and punished with those mischievious persons who put obstructions on the railroads.

But, to speak practically and as a citizen, unlike those who call themselves no-government men, I ask for, not *at once* no government, but at once a better government. Let every man make known what kind of government would command his respect, and that will be one step toward obtaining it.

After all, the practical reason why, when the power is once in the hands of the people, a majority are permitted, and for a long period continue, to rule is not because they are most likely to be in the right, nor because this seems fairest to the minority, but because they are physically the strongest. But a government in which the majority rule in all cases can not be based on justice, even as far as men understand it. Can there not be a government in which the majorities do not virtually decide right and wrong, but conscience?—in which majorities decide only those questions to which the rule of expediency is applicable? Must the citizen ever for a moment, or in the least degree, resign his conscience to the legislator? Why has every man a conscience then? I think that we should be men first, and subjects afterward. It is not desirable to cultivate a respect for the law, so much as for the right. The only obligation which I have a right to assume is to do at any time what I think right. It is truly enough said that a corporation has no conscience; but a corporation of conscientious men is a corporation *with* a conscience. Law never made men a whit more just; and, by means of their respect for it, even the well-disposed are daily made the agents on injustice. A common and natural result of an undue respect for the law is, that you may see a file of soldiers, colonel, captain, corporal, privates, powder-monkeys, and all, marching in admirable order over hill and dale to the wars, against their wills, ay, against their common sense and consciences, which makes it very steep marching indeed, and produces a palpitation of the heart. They have no doubt that it is a damnable business in which they are concerned; they are all peaceably inclined. Now, what are they? Men at all? or small movable forts and magazines, at the service of some unscrupulous man in power? Visit the Navy Yard, and behold a marine, such a man as an American government can make, or such as it can make a man with its black arts—a mere shadow and reminiscence of humanity, a man laid out alive and standing, and already, as one may say, buried under arms with funeral accompaniment, though it may be,

"Not a drum was heard, not a funeral note,
As his corse to the rampart we hurried;
Not a soldier discharged his farewell shot
O'er the grave where out hero was buried."

The mass of men serve the state thus, not as men mainly, but as machines, with their bodies. They are the standing army, and the militia, jailers, constables, posse comitatus, etc. In most cases there is no free exercise whatever of the judgement or of the moral sense; but they put themselves on a level with wood and earth and stones; and wooden men can perhaps be manufactured that will serve the purpose as well. Such command no more respect than men of straw or a lump of dirt. They have the same sort of worth only as horses and dogs. Yet such as these even are commonly esteemed good citizens. Others—as most legislators, politicians, lawyers, ministers, and office-holders—serve the state chiefly with their heads; and, as they rarely make any moral distinctions, they are as likely to serve the devil, without *intending* it, as God. A very few—as heroes, patriots, martyrs, reformers in the great sense, and *men*—serve the state with their consciences also, and so necessarily resist it for the most part; and they are commonly treated as enemies by it. A wise man will only be useful as a man, and will not submit to be "clay," and "stop a hole to keep the wind away," but leave that office to his dust at least:

"I am too high born to be propertied,
To be a second at control,
Or useful serving-man and instrument
To any sovereign state throughout the world."

He who gives himself entirely to his fellow men appears to them useless and selfish; but he who gives himself partially to them in pronounced a benefactor and philanthropist.

How does it become a man to behave toward the American government today? I answer, that he cannot without disgrace be associated with it. I cannot for an instant recognize that political organization as *my* government which is the *slave's* government also.

All men recognize the right of revolution; that is, the right to refuse allegiance to, and to resist, the government, when its tyranny or its inefficiency are great and unendurable. But almost all say that such is not the case now. But such was the case, they think, in the Revolution of '75. If one were to tell me that this was a bad government because it taxed certain foreign commodities brought to its ports, it is most probable that I should not make an ado about it, for I can do without them. All machines have their friction; and possibly this does enough good to counter-balance the evil. At any rate, it is a great evil to make a stir about it. But when the friction comes to have its machine, and oppression and robbery are organized, I say, let us not have such a machine any longer. In other words, when a sixth of the population of a nation which has undertaken to be the refuge of liberty are slaves, and a whole country is unjustly overrun and conquered by a foreign army, and subjected to military law, I think that it is not too soon for honest men to rebel and revolutionize. What makes this duty the more urgent is that fact that the country so overrun is not our own, but ours is the invading army.

Paley, a common authority with many on moral questions, in his chapter on the "Duty of Submission to Civil Government," resolves all civil obligation into expediency; and he proceeds to say that "so long as the interest of the whole society requires it, that is, so long as the established government cannot be resisted or changed without public inconvenience, it is the will of God . . . that the established government be obeyed—and no longer. This principle being admitted, the justice of every particular case of resistance is reduced to a computation of the quantity of the danger and grievance on the one side, and of the probability and expense of redressing it on the other." Of this, he says, every man shall judge for himself. But Paley appears never to have contemplated those cases to which the rule of expediency does not apply, in which a people, as well as an individual, must do justice, cost what it may. If I have unjustly wrested a plank from a drowning man, I must restore it to him though I drown myself. This, according to Paley, would be inconvenient. But he that would save his life, in such a case, shall lose it. This people must cease to hold slaves, and to make war on Mexico, though it cost them their existence as a people.

In their practice, nations agree with Paley; but does anyone think that Massachusetts does exactly what is right at the present crisis?

"A drab of stat,
a cloth-o'-silver slut,
To have her train borne up,
and her soul trail in the dirt."

Practically speaking, the opponents to a reform in Massachusetts are not a hundred thousand politicians at the South, but a hundred thousand merchants and farmers here, who are more interested in commerce and agriculture than they are in humanity, and are not prepared to do justice to the slave and to Mexico, *cost what it may*. I quarrel not with far-off foes, but with those who, near at home, co-operate with, and do the bidding of, those far away, and without whom the latter would be harmless. We are accustomed to say, that the mass of men are unprepared; but improvement is slow, because the few are not as materially wiser or better than the many. It is not so important that many should be good as you, as that there be some absolute goodness somewhere; for that will leaven the whole lump. There are thousands who are *in opinion* opposed to slavery and to the war, who yet in effect do nothing to put an end to them; who, esteeming themselves children of Washington and Franklin, sit down with their hands in their pockets, and say that they know not what to do, and do nothing; who even postpone the question of freedom to the question of free trade, and quietly read the prices-current along with the latest advices from Mexico, after dinner, and, it may be, fall asleep over them both. What is the price-current of an honest man and patriot today? They hesitate, and they regret, and sometimes they petition; but they do nothing in earnest and with effect. They will wait, well disposed, for other to remedy the evil, that they may no longer have it to regret. At most, they give up only a cheap vote, and a feeble countenance and Godspeed, to the right, as it goes by them. There are nine hundred and ninety-nine patrons of virtue to one virtuous man. But it is easier to deal with the real possessor of a thing than with the temporary guardian of it.

All voting is a sort of gaming, like checkers or backgammon, with a slight moral tinge to it, a playing with right and wrong, with moral questions; and betting naturally accompanies it. The character of the voters is not staked. I cast my vote, perchance, as I think right; but I am not vitally concerned that that right should prevail. I am willing to leave it to the majority. Its obligation, therefore, never exceeds that of expediency. Even *voting for the right* is *doing* nothing for it. It is only expressing to men feebly your desire that it should prevail. A wise man will not leave the right to the mercy of chance, nor wish it to prevail through the power of the majority. There is but little virtue in the action of masses of men. When the majority shall at length vote for the abolition of slavery, it will be because they are indifferent to slavery, or because there is but little slavery left to be abolished by their vote. *They* will then be the only slaves. Only *his* vote can hasten the abolition of slavery who asserts his own freedom by his vote.

I hear of a convention to be held at Baltimore, or elsewhere, for the selection of a candidate for the Presidency, made up chiefly of editors, and men who are politicians by profession; but I think, what is it to any independent, intelligent, and respectable man what decision they may come to? Shall we not have the advantage of this wisdom and honesty, nevertheless? Can we not count upon some independent votes? Are there not many individuals in the country who do not attend conventions? But no: I find that the respectable man, so called, has immediately drifted from his position, and despairs of his country, when his country has more reasons to despair of him. He forthwith adopts one of the candidates thus selected as the only *available* one, thus proving that he is himself *available* for any purposes of the demagogue. His vote is of no more worth than that of any unprincipled foreigner or hireling native, who may have been bought. O for a man who is a man, and, as my neighbor says, has a bone in his back which you cannot pass your hand through! Our statistics are at fault: the population has been returned too large. How many *men* are there to a square thousand miles in the country? Hardly one. Does not America offer any inducement for men to settle here? The American has dwindled into an Odd Fellow—one who may be known by the development of his organ of gregariousness, and a manifest lack of intellect and cheerful self-reliance; whose first and chief concern, on coming into the world, is to see that the almshouses are in good repair; and, before yet he has lawfully donned the virile garb, to collect a fund to the support of the widows and orphans that may be; who, in short, ventures to live only by the aid of the Mutual Insurance company, which has promised to bury him decently.

It is not a man's duty, as a matter of course, to devote himself to the eradication of any, even to most enormous wrong; he may still properly have other concerns to engage him; but it is his duty, at least, to wash his hands of it, and, if he gives it no thought longer, not to give it practically his support. If I devote myself to other pursuits and contemplations, I must first see, at least, that I do not pursue them sitting upon another man's shoulders. I must get off him first, that he may pursue his contemplations too. See what gross inconsistency is tolerated. I have heard some of my townsmen say, "I should like to have them order me out to help put down an insurrection of the slaves, or to march to Mexico—see if I would go"; and yet these very men have each, directly by their allegiance, and so indirectly, at least, by their money, furnished a substitute. The soldier is applauded who refuses to serve in an unjust war by those who do not refuse to sustain the unjust government which makes the war; is applauded by those whose own act and authority he disregards and sets at naught; as if the state were penitent to that degree that it hired one to scourge it while it sinned, but not to that degree that it left off sinning for a moment. Thus, under the name of Order and Civil Government, we are all made at last to pay homage to and support our own meanness. After the first blush of sin comes its indifference; and from immoral it becomes, as it were, unmoral, and not quite unnecessary to that life which we have made.

The broadest and most prevalent error requires the most disinterested virtue to sustain it. The slight reproach to which the virtue of patriotism is commonly liable, the noble are most likely to incur. Those who, while they disapprove of the character and measures of a government, yield to it their allegiance and support are undoubtedly its most conscientious supporters, and so frequently the most serious obstacles to reform. Some are petitioning the State to dissolve the Union, to disregard the requisitions of the President. Why do they not dissolve it themselves—the union between themselves and the State—and refuse to pay their quota into its treasury? Do not they stand in same relation to the State that the State does to the Union? And have not the same reasons prevented the State from resisting the Union which have prevented them from resisting the State?

How can a man be satisfied to entertain an opinion merely, and enjoy *it*? Is there any enjoyment in it, if his opinion is that he is aggrieved? If you are cheated out of a single dollar by your neighbor, you do not rest satisfied with knowing you are cheated, or with saying that you are cheated, or even with petitioning him to pay you your due; but you take effectual steps at once to obtain the full amount, and see to it that you are never cheated again. Action from principle, the perception and the performance of right, changes things and relations; it is essentially revolutionary, and does not consist wholly with anything which was. It not only divided States and churches, it divides families; ay, it divides the *individual*, separating the diabolical in him from the divine.

Unjust laws exist: shall we be content to obey them, or shall we endeavor to amend them, and obey them until we have succeeded, or shall we transgress them at once? Men, generally, under such a government as this, think that they ought to wait until they have persuaded the majority to alter them. They think that, if they should resist, the remedy would be worse than the evil. But it is the fault of the government itself that the remedy is worse than the evil. *It* makes it worse. Why is it not more apt to anticipate and provide for reform? Why does it not cherish its wise minority? Why does it cry and resist before it is hurt? Why does it not encourage its citizens to put out its faults, and *do* better than it would have them? Why does it always crucify Christ and excommunicate Copernicus and Luther, and pronounce Washington and Franklin rebels?

One would think, that a deliberate and practical denial of its authority was the only offense never contemplated by its government; else, why has it not assigned its definite, its suitable and proportionate, penalty? If a man who has no property refuses but once to earn nine shillings for the State, he is put in prison for a period unlimited by any law that I know, and determined only by the discretion of those who put him there; but if he should steal ninety times nine shillings from the State, he is soon permitted to go at large again.

If the injustice is part of the necessary friction of the machine of government, let it go, let it go: perchance it will wear smooth—certainly the machine will wear out. If the injustice has a spring, or a pulley, or a rope, or a crank, exclusively for itself, then perhaps you may consider whether the remedy will not be worse than the evil; but if it is of such a nature that it requires you to be the agent of injustice to another, then I say, break the law. Let your life be a counter-friction to stop the machine. What I have to do is to see, at any rate, that I do not lend myself to the wrong which I condemn.

As for adopting the ways of the State has provided for remedying the evil, I know not of such ways. They take too much time, and a man's life will be gone. I have other affairs to attend to. I came into this world, not chiefly to make this a good place to live in, but to live in it, be it good or bad. A man has not everything to do, but something; and because he cannot do *everything*, it is not necessary that he should be doing *something* wrong. It is not my business to be petitioning the Governor or the Legislature any more than it is theirs to petition me; and if they should not hear my petition, what should I do then? But in this case the State has provided no way: its very Constitution is the evil. This may seem to be harsh and stubborn and unconcilliatory; but it is to treat with the utmost kindness and consideration the only spirit that can appreciate or deserves it. So is all change for the better, like birth and death, which convulse the body.

I do not hesitate to say, that those who call themselves Abolitionists should at once effectually withdraw their support, both in person and property, from the government of Massachusetts, and not wait till they constitute a majority of one, before they suffer the right to prevail through them. I think that it is enough if they have God on their side, without waiting for that other one. Moreover, any man more right than his neighbors constitutes a majority of one already.

I meet this American government, or its representative, the State government, directly, and face to face, once a year—no more—in the person of its tax-gatherer; this is the only mode in which a man situated as I am necessarily meets it; and it then says distinctly, Recognize me; and the simplest, the most effectual, and, in the present posture of affairs, the indispensablest mode of treating with it on this head, of expressing your little satisfaction with and love for it, is to deny it then. My civil neighbor, the tax-gatherer, is the very man I have to deal with—for it is, after all, with men and not with parchment that I quarrel—and he has voluntarily chosen to be an agent of the government. How shall he ever know well that he is and does as an officer of the government, or as a man, until he is obliged to consider whether he will treat me, his neighbor, for whom he has respect, as a neighbor and well-disposed man, or as a maniac and disturber of the peace, and see if he can get over this obstruction to his neighborlines without a ruder and more impetuous thought or speech corresponding with his action. I know this well, that if one thousand, if one hundred, if ten men whom I could name—if ten *honest* men only—ay, if *one* HONEST man, in this State of Massachusetts, *ceasing to hold slaves*, were actually to withdraw from this co-partnership, and be locked up in the county jail therefor, it would be the abolition of slavery in America. For it matters not how small the beginning may seem to be: what is once well done is done forever. But we love better to talk about it: that we say is our mission. Reform keeps many scores of newspapers in its service, but not one man. If my esteemed neighbor, the State's ambassador, who will devote his days to the settlement of the question of human rights in the Council Chamber, instead of being threatened with the prisons of Carolina, were to sit down the prisoner of Massachusetts, that State which is so anxious to foist the sin of slavery upon her sister—though at present she can discover only an act of inhospitality to be the ground of a quarrel with her—the Legislature would not wholly waive the subject of the following winter.

Under a government which imprisons unjustly, the true place for a just man is also a prison. The proper place today, the only place which Massachusetts has provided for her freer and less despondent spirits, is in her prisons, to be put out and locked out of the State by her own act, as they have already put themselves out by their principles. It is there that the fugitive slave, and the Mexican prisoner on parole, and the Indian come to plead the wrongs of his race should find them; on that separate but more free and honorable ground, where the State places those who are not *with* her, but *against* her—the only house in a slave State in which a free man can abide with honor. If any think that their influence would be lost there, and their voices no longer afflict the ear of the State, that they would not be as an enemy within its walls, they do not know by how much truth is stronger than error, nor how much more eloquently and effectively he can combat injustice who has experienced a little in his own person. Cast your whole vote, not a strip of paper merely, but your whole influence. A minority is powerless while it conforms to the majority; it is not even a minority then; but it is irresistible when it clogs by its whole weight. If the alternative is to keep all just men in prison, or give up war and slavery, the State will not hesitate which to choose. If a thousand men were not to pay their tax bills this year, that would not be a violent and bloody measure, as it would be to pay them, and enable the State to commit violence and shed innocent blood. This is, in fact, the definition of a peaceable revolution, if any such is possible. If the tax-gatherer, or any other public officer, asks me, as one has done, "But what shall I do?" my answer is, "If you really wish to do anything, resign your office." When the subject has refused allegiance, and the officer has resigned from office, then the revolution is accomplished. But even suppose blood should flow. Is there not a sort of blood shed when the conscience is wounded? Through this wound a man's real manhood and immortality flow out, and he bleeds to an everlasting death. I see this blood flowing now.

I have contemplated the imprisonment of the offender, rather than the seizure of his goods—though both will serve the same purpose—because they who assert the purest right, and consequently are most dangerous to a corrupt State, commonly have not spent much time in accumulating property. To such the State renders comparatively small service, and a slight tax is wont to appear exorbitant, particularly if they are obliged to earn it by special labor with their hands. If there were one who lived wholly without the use of money, the State itself would hesitate to demand it of him. But the rich man—not to make any invidious comparison—is always sold to the institution which makes him rich. Absolutely speaking, the more money, the less virtue; for money comes between a man and his objects, and obtains them for him; it was certainly no great virtue to obtain it. It puts to rest many questions which he would otherwise be taxed to answer; while the only new question which it puts is the hard but superfluous one, how to spend it. Thus his moral ground is taken from under his feet. The opportunities of living are diminished in proportion as that are called the "means" are increased. The best thing a man can do for his culture when he is rich is to endeavor to carry out those schemes which he entertained when he was poor. Christ answered the Herodians according to their condition. "Show me the tribute-money," said he—and one took a penny out of his pocket—if you use money which has the image of Caesar on it, and which he has made current and valuable, that is, *if you are men of the State*, and gladly enjoy the advantages of Caesar's government, then pay him back some of his own when he demands it. "Render therefore to Caesar that which is Caesar's and to God those things which are God's"—leaving them no wiser than before as to which was which; for they did not wish to know.

When I converse with the freest of my neighbors, I perceive that, whatever they may say about the magnitude and seriousness of the question, and their regard for the public tranquillity, the long and the short of the matter is, that they cannot spare the protection of the existing government, and they dread the consequences to their property and families of disobedience to it. For my own part, I should not like to think that I ever rely on the protection of the State. But, if I deny the authority of the State when it presents its tax bill, it will soon take and waste all my property, and so harass me and my children without end. This is hard. This makes it impossible for a man to live honestly, and at the same time comfortably, in outward respects. It will not be worth the while to accumulate property; that would be sure to go again. You must hire or squat somewhere, and raise but a small crop, and eat that soon. You must live within yourself, and depend upon yourself always tucked up and ready for a start, and not have many affairs. A man may grow rich in Turkey even, if he will be in all respects a good subject of the Turkish government. Confucius said: "If a state is governed by the principles of reason, poverty and misery are subjects of shame; if a state is not governed by the principles of reason, riches and honors are subjects of shame." No: until I want the protection of Massachusetts to be extended to me in some distant Southern port, where my liberty is endangered, or until I am bent solely on building up an estate at home by peaceful enterprise, I can afford to refuse allegiance to Massachusetts, and her right to my property and life. It costs me less in every sense to incur the penalty of disobedience to the State than it would to obey. I should feel as if I were worth less in that case.

Some years ago, the State met me in behalf of the Church, and commanded me to pay a certain sum toward the support of a clergyman whose preaching my father attended, but never I myself. "Pay," it said, "or be locked up in the jail." I declined to pay. But, unfortunately, another man saw fit to pay it. I did not see why the schoolmaster should be taxed to support the priest, and not the priest the schoolmaster; for I was not the State's schoolmaster, but I supported myself by voluntary subscription. I did not see why the lyceum should not present its tax bill, and have the State to back its demand, as well as the Church. However, at the request of the selectmen, I condescended to make some such statement as this in writing: "Know all men by these presents, that I, Henry Thoreau, do not wish to be regarded as a member of any incorporated society which I have not joined." This I gave to the town clerk; and he has it. The State, having thus learned that I did not wish to be regarded as a member of that church, has never made a like demand on me since; though it said that it must adhere to its original presumption that time. If I had known how to name them, I should then have signed off in detail from all the societies which I never signed on to; but I did not know where to find such a complete list.

I have paid no poll tax for six years. I was put into a jail once on this account, for one night; and, as I stood considering the walls of solid stone, two or three feet thick, the door of wood and iron, a foot thick, and the iron grating which strained the light, I could not help being struck with the foolishness of that institution which treated me as if I were mere flesh and blood and bones, to be locked up. I wondered that it should have concluded at length that this was the best use it could put me to, and had never thought to avail itself of my services in some way. I saw that, if there was a wall of stone between me and my townsmen, there was a still more difficult one to climb or break through before they could get to be as free as I was. I did nor for a moment feel confined, and the walls seemed a great waste of stone and mortar. I felt as if I alone of all my townsmen had paid my tax. They plainly did not know how to treat me, but behaved like persons who are underbred. In every threat and in every compliment there was a blunder; for they thought that my chief desire was to stand the other side of that stone wall. I could not but smile to see how industriously they locked the door on my meditations, which followed them out again without let or hindrance, and *they* were really all that was dangerous. As they could not reach me, they had resolved to punish my body; just as boys, if they cannot come at some person against whom they have a spite, will abuse his dog. I saw that the State was half-witted, that it was timid as a lone woman with her silver spoons, and that it did not know its friends from its foes, and I lost all my remaining respect for it, and pitied it.

Thus the state never intentionally confronts a man's sense, intellectual or moral, but only his body, his senses. It is not armed with superior wit or honesty, but with superior physical strength. I was not born to be forced. I will breathe after my own fashion. Let us see who is the strongest. What force has a multitude? They only can force me who obey a higher law than I. They force me to become like themselves. I do not hear of *men* being *forced* to live this way or that by masses of men. What sort of life were that to live? When I meet a government which says to me, "Your money or your life," why should I be in haste to give it my money? It may be in a great strait, and not know what to do: I cannot help that. It must help itself; do as I do. It is not worth the while to snivel about it. I am not responsible for the successful working of the machinery of society. I am not the son of the engineer. I perceive that, when an acorn and a chestnut fall side by side, the one does not remain inert to make way for the other, but both obey their own laws, and spring and grow and flourish as best they can, till one, perchance, overshadows and destroys the other. If a plant cannot live according to nature, it dies; and so a man.

The night in prison was novel and interesting enough. The prisoners in their shirtsleeves were enjoying a chat and the evening air in the doorway, when I entered. But the jailer said, "Come, boys, it is time to lock up"; and so they dispersed, and I heard the sound of their steps returning into the hollow apartments. My room-mate was introduced to me by the jailer as "a first-rate fellow and clever man." When the door was locked, he showed me where to hang my hat, and how he managed matters there. The rooms were whitewashed once a month; and this one, at least, was the whitest, most simply furnished, and probably neatest apartment in town. He naturally wanted to know where I came from, and what brought me there; and, when I had told him, I asked him in my turn how he came there, presuming him to be an honest man, of course; and as the world goes, I believe he was. "Why," said he, "they accuse me of burning a barn; but I never did it." As near as I could discover, he had probably gone to bed in a barn when drunk, and smoked his pipe there; and so a barn was burnt. He had the reputation of being a clever man, had been there some three months waiting for his trial to come on, and would have to wait as much longer; but he was quite domesticated and contented, since he got his board for nothing, and thought that he was well treated.

He occupied one window, and I the other; and I saw that if one stayed there long, his principal business would be to look out the window. I had soon read all the tracts that were left there, and examined where former prisoners had broken out, and where a grate had been sawed off, and heard the history of the various occupants of that room; for I found that even there there was a history and a gossip which never circulated beyond the walls of the jail. Probably this is the only house in the town where verses are composed, which are afterward printed in a circular form, but not published. I was shown quite a long list of young men who had been detected in an attempt to escape, who avenged themselves by singing them.

I pumped my fellow-prisoner as dry as I could, for fear I should never see him again; but at length he showed me which was my bed, and left me to blow out the lamp.

It was like travelling into a far country, such as I had never expected to behold, to lie there for one night. It seemed to me that I never had heard the town clock strike before, not the evening sounds of the village; for we slept with the windows open, which were inside the grating. It was to see my native village in the light of the Middle Ages, and our Concord was turned into a Rhine stream, and visions of knights and castles passed before me. They were the voices of old burghers that I heard in the streets. I was an involuntary spectator and auditor of whatever was done and said in the kitchen of the adjacent village inn—a wholly new and rare experience to me. It was a closer view of my native town. I was fairly inside of it. I never had seen its institutions before. This is one of its peculiar institutions; for it is a shire town. I began to comprehend what its inhabitants were about.

In the morning, our breakfasts were put through the hole in the door, in small oblong-square tin pans, made to fit, and holding a pint of chocolate, with brown bread, and an iron spoon. When they called for the vessels again, I was green enough to return what bread I had left, but my comrade seized it, and said that I should lay that up for lunch or dinner. Soon after he was let out to work at haying in a neighboring field, whither he went every day, and would not be back till noon; so he bade me good day, saying that he doubted if he should see me again.

When I came out of prison—for some one interfered, and paid that tax —I did not perceive that great changes had taken place on the common, such as he observed who went in a youth and emerged a gray-headed man; and yet a change had come to my eyes come over the scene—the town, and State, and country, greater than any that mere time could effect. I saw yet more distinctly the State in which I lived. I saw to what extent the people among whom I lived could be trusted as good neighbors and friends; that their friendship was for summer weather only; that they did not greatly propose to do right; that they were a distinct race from me by their prejudices and superstitions, as the Chinamen and Malays are; that in their sacrifices to humanity they ran no risks, not even to their property; that after all they were not so noble but they treated the thief as he had treated them, and hoped, by a certain outward observance and a few prayers, and by walking in a particular straight though useless path from time to time, to save their souls. This may be to judge my neighbors harshly; for I believe that many of them are not aware that they have such an institution as the jail in their village.

It was formerly the custom in our village, when a poor debtor came out of jail, for his acquaintances to salute him, looking through their fingers, which were crossed to represent the jail window, "How do ye do?" My neighbors did not thus salute me, but first looked at me, and then at one another, as if I had returned from a long journey. I was put into jail as I was going to the shoemaker's to get a shoe which was mended. When I was let out the next morning, I proceeded to finish my errand, and, having put on my mended shoe, joined a huckleberry party, who were impatient to put themselves under my conduct; and in half an hour—for the horse was soon tackled—was in the midst of a huckleberry field, on one of our highest hills, two miles off, and then the State was nowhere to be seen.

This is the whole history of "My Prisons."

I have never declined paying the highway tax, because I am as desirous of being a good neighbor as I am of being a bad subject; and as for supporting schools, I am doing my part to educate my fellow countrymen now. It is for no particular item in the tax bill that I refuse to pay it. I simply wish to refuse allegiance to the State, to withdraw and stand aloof from it effectually. I do not care to trace the course of my dollar, if I could, till it buys a man or a musket to shoot one with—the dollar is innocent—but I am concerned to trace the effects of my allegiance. In fact, I quietly declare war with the State, after my fashion, though I will still make use and get what advantages of her I can, as is usual in such cases.

If others pay the tax which is demanded of me, from a sympathy with the State, they do but what they have already done in their own case, or rather they abet injustice to a greater extent than the State requires. If they pay the tax from a mistaken interest in the individual taxed, to save his property, or prevent his going to jail, it is because they have not considered wisely how far they let their private feelings interfere with the public good.

This, then, is my position at present. But one cannot be too much on his guard in such a case, lest his actions be biased by obstinacy or an undue regard for the opinions of men. Let him see that he does only what belongs to himself and to the hour.

I think sometimes, Why, this people mean well, they are only ignorant; they would do better if they knew how: why give your neighbors this pain to treat you as they are not inclined to? But I think again, This is no reason why I should do as they do, or permit others to suffer much greater pain of a different kind. Again, I sometimes say to myself, When many millions of men, without heat, without ill will, without personal feelings of any kind, demand of you a few shillings only, without the possibility, such is their constitution, of retracting or altering their present demand, and without the possibility, on your side, of appeal to any other millions, why expose yourself to this overwhelming brute force? You do not resist cold and hunger, the winds and the waves, thus obstinately; you quietly submit to a thousand similar necessities. You do not put your head into the fire. But just in proportion as I regard this as not wholly a brute force, but partly a human force, and consider that I have relations to those millions as to so many millions of men, and not of mere brute or inanimate things, I see that appeal is possible, first and instantaneously, from them to the Maker of them, and, secondly, from them to themselves. But if I put my head deliberately into the fire, there is no appeal to fire or to the Maker of fire, and I have only myself to blame. If I could convince myself that I have any right to be satisfied with men as they are, and to treat them accordingly, and not according, in some respects, to my requisitions and expectations of what they and I ought to be, then, like a good Mussulman and fatalist, I should endeavor to be satisfied with things as they are, and say it is the will of God. And, above all, there is this difference between resisting this and a purely brute or natural force, that I can resist this with some effect; but I cannot expect, like Orpheus, to change the nature of the rocks and trees and beasts.

I do not wish to quarrel with any man or nation. I do not wish to split hairs, to make fine distinctions, or set myself up as better than my neighbors. I seek rather, I may say, even an excuse for conforming to the laws of the land. I am but too ready to conform to them. Indeed, I have reason to suspect myself on this head; and each year, as the tax-gatherer comes round, I find myself disposed to review the acts and position of the general and State governments, and the spirit of the people to discover a pretext for conformity.

"We must affect our country as our parents,
And if at any time we alienate

Out love or industry from doing it honor,
We must respect effects and teach the soul
Matter of conscience and religion,
And not desire of rule or benefit."

I believe that the State will soon be able to take all my work of this sort out of my hands, and then I shall be no better patriot than my fellow-countrymen. Seen from a lower point of view, the Constitution, with all its faults, is very good; the law and the courts are very respectable; even this State and this American government are, in many respects, very admirable, and rare things, to be thankful for, such as a great many have described them; seen from a higher still, and the highest, who shall say what they are, or that they are worth looking at or thinking of at all?

However, the government does not concern me much, and I shall bestow the fewest possible thoughts on it. It is not many moments that I live under a government, even in this world. If a man is thought-free, fancy-free, imagination-free, that which *is not* never for a long time appearing *to be* to him, unwise rulers or reformers cannot fatally interrupt him.

I know that most men think differently from myself; but those whose lives are by profession devoted to the study of these or kindred subjects content me as little as any. Statesmen and legislators, standing so completely within the institution, never distinctly and nakedly behold it. They speak of moving society, but have no resting-place without it. They may be men of a certain experience and discrimination, and have no doubt invented ingenious and even useful systems, for which we sincerely thank them; but all their wit and usefulness lie within certain not very wide limits. They are wont to forget that the world is not governed by policy and expediency. Webster never goes behind government, and so cannot speak with authority about it. His words are wisdom to those legislators who contemplate no essential reform in the existing government; but for thinkers, and those who legislate for all time, he never once glances at the subject. I know of those whose serene and wise speculations on this theme would soon reveal the limits of his mind's range and hospitality. Yet, compared with the cheap professions of most reformers, and the still cheaper wisdom an eloquence of politicians in general, his are almost the only sensible and valuable words, and we thank Heaven for him. Comparatively, he is always strong, original, and, above all, practical. Still, his quality is not wisdom, but prudence. The lawyer's truth is not Truth, but consistency or a consistent expediency. Truth is always in harmony with herself, and is not concerned chiefly to reveal the justice that may consist with wrong-doing. He well deserves to be called, as he has been called, the Defender of the Constitution. There are really no blows to be given him but defensive ones. He is not a leader, but a follower. His leaders are the men of '87. "I have never made an effort," he says, "and never propose to make an effort; I have never countenanced an effort, and never mean to countenance an effort, to disturb the arrangement as originally made, by which various States came into the Union." Still thinking of the sanction which the Constitution gives to slavery, he says, "Because it was part of the original compact—let it stand." Notwithstanding his special acuteness and ability, he is unable to take a fact out of its merely political relations, and behold it as it lies absolutely to be disposed of by the intellect—what, for instance, it behooves a man to do here in American today with regard to slavery—but ventures, or is driven, to make some such desperate answer to the following, while professing to speak absolutely, and as a private man—from which what new and singular of social duties might be inferred? "The manner," says he, "in which the governments of the States where slavery exists are to regulate it is for their own consideration, under the responsibility to their constituents, to the general laws of propriety, humanity, and justice, and to God. Associations formed elsewhere, springing from a feeling of humanity, or any other cause, have nothing whatever to do with it. They have never received any encouragement from me and they never will." [These extracts have been inserted since the lecture was read -HDT]

They who know of no purer sources of truth, who have traced up its stream no higher, stand, and wisely stand, by the Bible and the Constitution, and drink at it there with reverence and humanity; but they who behold where it comes trickling into this lake or that pool, gird up their loins once more, and continue their pilgrimage toward its fountainhead.

No man with a genius for legislation has appeared in America. They are rare in the history of the world. There are orators, politicians, and eloquent men, by the thousand; but the speaker has not yet opened his mouth to speak who is capable of settling the much-vexed questions of the day. We love eloquence for its own sake, and not for any truth which it may utter, or any heroism it may inspire. Our legislators have not yet learned the comparative value of free trade and of freedom, of union, and of rectitude, to a nation. They have no genius or talent for comparatively humble questions of taxation and finance, commerce and manufactures and agriculture. If we were left solely to the wordy wit of legislators in Congress for our guidance, uncorrected by the seasonable experience and the effectual complaints of the people, America would not long retain her rank among the nations. For eighteen hundred years, though perchance I have no right to say it, the New Testament has been written; yet where is the legislator who has wisdom and practical talent enough to avail himself of the light which it sheds on the science of legislation.

The authority of government, even such as I am willing to submit to— for I will cheerfully obey those who know and can do better than I, and in many things even those who neither know nor can do so well—is still an impure one: to be strictly just, it must have the sanction and consent of the governed. It can have no pure right over my person and property but what I concede to it. The progress from an absolute to a limited monarchy, from a limited monarchy to a democracy, is a progress toward a true respect for the individual. Even the Chinese philosopher was wise enough to regard the individual as the basis of the empire. Is a democracy, such as we know it, the last improvement possible in government? Is it not possible to take a step further towards recognizing and organizing the rights of man? There will never be a really free and enlightened State until the State comes to recognize the individual as a higher and independent power, from which all its own power and authority are derived, and treats him accordingly. I please myself with imagining a State at last which can afford to be just to all men, and to treat the individual with respect as a neighbor; which even would not think it inconsistent with its own repose if a few were to live aloof from it, not meddling with it, nor embraced by it, who fulfilled all the duties of neighbors and fellow men. A State which bore this kind of fruit, and suffered it to drop off as fast as it ripened, would prepare the way for a still more perfect and glorious State, which I have also imagined, but not yet anywhere seen.

"LIFE, LIBERTY, AND PROPERTY"
DO NOT EXIST BECAUSE MEN HAVE MADE LAWS."

FREDERIC BASTIAT

"OUR IDEAS OF FREEDOM ARE THE MOST POWERFUL POLITICAL WEAPONS MAN HAS EVER FORGED."

WILLIAM O. DOUGLASS

Annotated History of Defiance

by: Darryl W. Perry

"Free men stand against a tyrant"
was the proclamation of Leonidas
His brave 300 saw their end
But their homes, they did defend.

In one last act of defiance
"FREEDOM!" was the cry from William Wallace

"Liberty or Death" was Patrick Henry's request
The British troops did their best
to deliver to him the latter
in the process much blood did splatter.
Twas the blood of tyrants and patriots,
for the Tree of Liberty, blood waters it.

"Don't tread on me!"
a motto for the Sons of Liberty.
From those before us to those yet to come
we are all brothers and sisters of freedom.
You should always remember this
"Your heart is free, have the courage to follow it!"

"DEATH IS BETTER,
A MILDER FATE THAN TYRANNY."

AESCHYLUS

Independence: A Solemn Duty

by: Richard Henry Lee

The time will certainly come when the fated separation between the mother country and these colonies must take place whether you will or no, for it is so decreed by the very nature of things by the progressive increase of our population, the fertility of our soil, the extent of our territory, the industry of our countrymen, and the immensity of the ocean which separates the two countries. And if this be true, as it is most true, who does not see that the sooner it takes place, the better? -- that it would be the height of folly not to seize the present occasion when British injustice has filled all hearts with indignation, inspired all minds with courage, united all opinions in one, and put arms in every hand? And how long must we traverse three thousand miles of a stormy sea to solicit of arrogant and insolent men either counsel or commands to regulate our domestic affairs? From what we have already achieved it is easy to presume what we shall hereafter accomplish. Experience is the source of sage counsels and liberty is the mother of great men. Have you not seen the enemy driven from Lexington by citizens armed and assembled in one day? Already their most celebrated generals have yielded in Boston to the skill of ours. Already their seamen repulsed from our coasts wander over the ocean, the sport of tempests and the prey of famine. Let us hail the favorable omen and fight not for the sake of knowing on what terms we are to be the slaves of England but to secure to ourselves a free existence to found a just and independent government.

Why do we longer delay? why still deliberate? Let this most happy day give birth to the American Republic. Let her arise not to devastate and conquer but to re-establish the reign of peace and the laws. The eyes of Europe are fixed upon us; she demands of us a living example of freedom that may contrast by the felicity of her citizens with the ever increasing tyranny which desolates her polluted shores. She invites us to prepare an asylum where the unhappy may find solace and the persecuted repose. She entreats us to cultivate a propitious soil where that generous plant which first sprang up and grew in England but is now withered by the poisonous blasts of Scottish tyranny may revive and flourish, sheltering under its salubrious and interminable shade all the unfortunate of the human race. This is the end presaged by so many omens; by our first victories; by the present ardor and union; by the flight of Howe and the pestilence which broke out among Dunmore's people; by the very winds which baffled the enemy's fleets and transports, and that terrible tempest which engulfed seven hundred vessels upon the coast of Newfoundland. If we are not this day wanting in our duty to our country, the names of the American legislators will be placed, by posterity, at the side of those of Theseus, of Lycurgus, of Romulus of Numa, of the three Williams of Nassau, and of all those whose memory has been and will be forever dear to virtuous men and good citizens.

"THE RIGHT TO BE LET ALONE IS
INDEED THE BEGINNING OF ALL FREEDOM."

WILLIAM O. DOUGLASS

"THE PROVERB WARNS THAT
'YOU SHOULD NOT BITE
THE HAND THAT FEEDS YOU.'
BUT MAYBE YOU SHOULD
IF IT PREVENTS YOU
FROM FEEDING YOURSELF."

THOMAS SZASZ

The Tax Poem

by: anonymous

Tax his land,
Tax his bed,
Tax the table
At which he's fed.

Tax his tractor,
Tax his mule,
Teach him taxes
Are the rule.

Tax his work,
Tax his pay,
He works for peanuts
Anyway!

Tax his cow,
Tax his goat,
Tax his pants,
Tax his coat.

Tax his ties,
Tax his shirt,
Tax his work,
Tax his dirt.

Tax his tobacco,
Tax his drink,
Tax him if he
Tries to think.

Tax his cigars,
Tax his beers,

If he cries
Tax his tears.

Tax his car,
Tax his gas,
Find other ways
To tax his .....

Tax all he has
Then let him know
That you won't be done
Till he has no dough.

When he screams and hollers;
Then tax him some more,
Tax him till
He's good and sore.

Then tax his coffin,
Tax his grave,
Tax the sod in
Which he's laid.

Put these words
Upon his tomb,
'Taxes drove me
to my doom....'

When he's gone,
Do not relax,
Its time to apply
The inheritance tax.

Accounts Receivable Tax
Building Permit Tax

CDL license Tax
Cigarette Tax
Corporate Income Tax
Dog License Tax
Excise Taxes
Federal Income Tax
Federal Unemployment Tax (FUTA)
Fishing License Tax
Food License Tax
Fu el Permit Tax
Gasoline Tax (44.75 cents per gallon)
Gross Receipts Tax
Hunting License Tax
Inheritance Tax
Inventory Tax
IRS Interest Charges IRS Penalties (tax on top of tax)
Liquor Tax
Luxury Taxes
Marriage License Tax
Medicare Tax
Personal Property Tax
Property Tax
Real Estate Tax
Service Charge T ax
Social Security Tax
Road Usage Tax
Sales Tax
Recreational20Vehicle Tax
School Tax
State Income Tax
State Unemployment Tax (SUTA)
Telephone Federal Excise Tax
Telephone Federal Universal Service Fee Tax
Telephone Federal, State and Local Surcharge Taxes
Telephone Minimum Usage Surcharge Tax
Telephone Recurring and Non-recurring Charges Tax
Telephone state and Local Tax

Telephone Usage Charge Tax
Utility Taxes
Vehicle License Registration Tax
Vehicle Sales Tax
Watercraft Registration Tax
Well Permit Tax
Workers Compensation Tax

Still think this is funny?

"IT IS WELL ENOUGH THAT PEOPLE
OF THE NATION DO NOT UNDERSTAND
OUR BANKING AND MONETARY SYSTEM,
FOR IF THEY DID, I BELIEVE THERE WOULD BE
A REVOLUTION BEFORE TOMORROW MORNING."

HENRY FORD

"WITHOUT FREEDOM OF THOUGHT,
THERE CAN BE NO SUCH THING AS WISDOM;
AND NO SUCH THING AS PUBLIC LIBERTY,
WITHOUT FREEDOM OF SPEECH."

CATO

The Present Crisis

by: James Russell Lowell

When a deed is done for Freedom, through the broad earth's aching breast
Runs a thrill of joy prophetic, trembling on from east to west,
And the slave, where'er he cowers, feels the soul within him climb
To the awful verge of manhood, as the energy sublime
Of a century bursts full-blossomed on the thorny stem of Time.

Through the walls of hut and palace shoots the instantaneous throe,
When the travail of the Ages wrings earth's systems to and fro;
At the birth of each new Era, with a recognizing start,
Nation wildly looks at nation, standing with mute lips apart,
And glad Truth's yet mightier man-child leaps beneath the Future's heart.

So the Evil's triumph sendeth, with a terror and a chill,
Under continent to continent, the sense of coming ill,
And the slave, where'er he cowers, feels his sympathies with God
In hot tear-drops ebbing earthward, to be drunk up by the sod,
Till a corpse crawls round unburied, delving in the nobler clod.

For mankind are one in spirit, and an instinct bears along,
Round the earth's electric circle, the swift flash of right or wrong;
Whether conscious or unconscious, yet Humanity's vast frame
Through its ocean-sundered fibres feels the gush of joy or shame;--
In the gain or loss of one race all the rest have equal claim.

Once to every man and nation comes the moment to decide,
In the strife of Truth with Falsehood, for the good or evil side;
Some great cause, God's new Messiah, offering each the bloom or blight,
Parts the goats upon the left hand, and the sheep upon the right,
And the choice goes by forever 'twixt that darkness and that light.

Hast thou chosen, O my people, on whose party thou shalt stand,
Ere the Doom from its worn sandals shakes the dust against our land?
Though the cause of Evil prosper, yet 'tis Truth alone is strong,
And, albeit she wander outcast now, I see around her throng
Troops of beautiful, tall angels, to enshield her from all wrong.

Backward look across the ages and the beacon-moments see,

That, like peaks of some sunk continent, jut through Oblivion's sea;
Not an ear in court or market for the low foreboding cry
Of those Crises, God's stern winnowers, from whose feet earth's chaff
    must fly;
Never shows the choice momentous till the judgment hath passed by.

Careless seems the great Avenger; history's pages but record
One death-grapple in the darkness 'twixt old systems and the Word;
Truth forever on the scaffold, Wrong forever on the throne,--
Yet that scaffold sways the future, and, behind the dim unknown,
Standeth God within the shadow, keeping watch above his own.

We see dimly in the Present what is small and what is great.
Slow of faith how weak an arm may turn the iron helm of fate,
But the soul is still oracular; amid the market's din.
List the ominous stern whisper from the Delphic cave within,--
'They enslave their children's children who make compromise with sin.'

Slavery, the earth-born Cyclops, fellest of the giant brood,
Sons of brutish Force and Darkness, who have drenched the earth with
    blood,
Famished in his self-made desert, blinded by our purer day,
Gropes in yet unblasted regions for his miserable prey;--
Shall we guide his gory fingers where our helpless children play?

Then to side with Truth is noble when we share her wretched crust,
Ere her cause bring fame and profit, and 'tis prosperous to be just;
Then it is the brave man chooses, while the coward stands aside,
Doubting in his abject spirit, till his Lord is crucified,
And the multitude make virtue of the faith they had denied.

Count me o'er earth's chosen heroes,--they were souls that stood alone,
While the men they agonized for hurled the contumelious stone,
Stood serene, and down the future saw the golden beam incline
To the side of perfect justice, mastered by their faith divine,
By one man's plain truth to manhood and to God's supreme design.

By the light of burning heretics Christ's bleeding feet I track,
Toiling up new Calvaries ever with the cross that turns not back,
And these mounts of anguish number how each generation learned
One new word of that grand Credo which in prophet-hearts hath burned
Since the first man stood God-conquered with his face to heaven upturned.

For Humanity sweeps onward: where to-day the martyr stands,
On the morrow crouches Judas with the silver in his hands;
Far in front the cross stands ready and the crackling fagots burn,
While the hooting mob of yesterday in silent awe return
To glean up the scattered ashes into History's golden urn.

'Tis as easy to be heroes as to sit the idle slaves
Of a legendary virtue carved upon our fathers' graves,
Worshippers of light ancestral make the present light a crime;--
Was the Mayflower launched by cowards, steered by men behind their
    time?
Turn those tracks toward Past or Future that make Plymouth Rock
    sublime?

They were men of present valor, stalwart old iconoclasts,
Unconvinced by axe or gibbet that all virtue was the Past's;
But we make their truth our falsehood, thinking that hath made us free.
Hoarding it in mouldy parchments, while our tender spirits flee
The rude grasp of that great Impulse which drove them across the sea.

They have rights who dare maintain them; we are traitors to our sires,
Smothering in their holy ashes Freedom's new-lit altar-fires;
Shall we make their creed our jailer? Shall we, in our haste to slay,
From the tombs of the old prophets steal the funeral lamps away
To light up the martyr-fagots round the prophets of to-day?

New occasions teach new duties; Time makes ancient good uncouth;
They must upward still, and onward, who would keep abreast of Truth;
Lo, before us gleam her camp-fires! we ourselves must Pilgrims be,
Launch our Mayflower, and steer boldly through the desperate winter sea,
Nor attempt the Future's portal with the Past's blood-rusted key.

"EXTREMISM IN DEFENSE
OF LIBERTY IS NO VICE.
TOLERANCE IN THE FACE
OF TYRANNY IS NO VIRTUE."

BARRY GOLDWATER

I'm a Domestic Terrorist

by: Adam Kokesh
March 28, 2009

Right now, I am listening to Tom Woods at the first Campaign for Liberty regional conference in St Louis. They think we're terrorists here. A report recently released by the Missouri Information Analysis Center equates Ron Paul supporters, tax resistors, militia members, and flyers of the Gadsden flag as "terrorists."

According to Merriam-Webster, terrorism is " the systematic use of terror especially as a means of coercion." It also defines terror as "a state of intense fear." The definition that I learned in school is even more specific: the threat or use of violence to incite fear by non-state actors to influence the actions or policies of governments."

So terrorism can go two ways in directing its threat or use of violence, by either terrorizing a population or terrorizing the government directly. The moral choice is to attack the transgressors of individual rights, the violators of the peace, and the organized criminals that are always to be found within the government, and not in the general population. What more righteous cause could there be than to strike fear into the hearts of those who think and act like they can control by force the lives of others?

As a political movement, we are calling out the abusers of power, the tramplers of the Constitution, the servants and lackeys of the truly powerful, and we want them to be afraid! We want them to be afraid first because we are a political force. We are young, we are strong, we are calling for no less than a revolution, and we are not going anywhere until we get it!

The revolution that we speak of is a revolution of values, a paradigm shift, and a renewed commitment among the American people to patriotism, not loyalism. Our patriotism is resisting state power and being ever-ready to defend this country . . . from the government. This is in direct opposition to the current propaganda driven definition that has perverted patriotism into loyalism, the worship of power and authority and willingness to cede the rights of self-ownership to an external power that is the source of all unjust powers in the world. As a political force, they should fear us.

The core of our philosophy is non-aggression, but we do not cede the right to self-defense and collective self-defense. As Judge Napolitano said here just last night, "The dirty little secret about the second amendment, is that it was written that way so that you could shoot at the government!" The assertion of the human right, the natural right, or God-given right, to keep and bear arms is the utmost manifestation of that old rallying cry, "POWER TO THE PEOPLE!"

Thomas Jefferson said, "The strongest reason for the people to retain the right to keep and bear arms is, as a last resort, to protect themselves against tyranny in government." We live in an era of uncanny increases in tyranny in the United States and never has it been more important, despite the heightened difficulty, to assert the right to keep and bear arms. John F. Kennedy astutely observed, "Those who make peaceful revolution impossible will make violent revolution inevitable."

To go back to Jefferson, "The tree of liberty must be refreshed from time to time with the blood of patriots and tyrants." Make no mistake, the first blood of this era's revolution has already been spilled. The victims of a violent statism are all around us. We are far from ruling out the possibility of peaceful revolution, but we bring that same commitment that our founders did to today's cause of liberty, and if you would use the force of government to trample the rights of others, you should be very, very afraid!

If you want to be respected as an individual, if you want to respect the rights of others, you have nothing to fear. If you believe that our government is no longer serving the people, join us. As a member of this movement I am fighting for no less than the highest values of humanity that this country was founded on. That makes me a patriot. Some of us found out the hard way that the greatest enemies of the Constitution that I celebrate only as a means of restraining government power, are not to be found in the sands of some far off land, but rather right here at home. We know who our common enemies really are, and I want them to be scared. So I guess that makes me a terrorist. I am a domestic terrorist for freedom!

"FREEDOM IS NOT A GIFT RECEIVED
FROM THE STATE OR LEADER,
BUT A POSSESSION TO BE WON
EVERY DAY BY THE EFFORT OF
EACH AND THE UNION OF ALL."

ALBERT CAMUS

"ALL THAT IS NECESSARY FOR EVIL TO TRIUMPH,

IS FOR GOOD MEN TO DO NOTHING."

EDMUND BURKE

The Future and Friends

by Brandon Trent

Not often now days do I get excited at the prospect of facing the Future.
The few times that I do get excited the prospect doesn't seem to last very
long
Over the past year I've met and befriended many many people
who share like interests and goals.
Some are young; some are old;
they come from all races and all ethnic backgrounds;
but it is what we have in common that makes us so close.
Among friends; especially those whom share your likes, goals, hopes and
even fears of the Future
discussion comes easy and quick.
Topics of discussion may vary;
they may be light or in most cases heavy;
but they all have one thing in common;
they set common goals and thoughts for the Future.
Those starting out on their journey of life may seek a lasting relationship
of love;
those who are old may seek reunion with loves already gone on from this
travel;
though the ends are different the goals for the Future are the same.
Friends make the prospect of the Future less frightening and less
troublesome.
Friends are always there to bounce ideas off of,
work alongside, care for, just in general to be there.
That makes things less uncertain and less frightening.
Yes while the Future frightens me;
I along with my friends and family will stand strong in the face of
adversity.
We will stand strong in the face of tyranny and oppression;
we will live on and we will be strong.
For with friends the Future isn't so troublesome after all.

"HE IS THE FREEMAN
WHOM THE TRUTH MAKES FREE."

WILLIAM COWPER

Freedom Song

by: Kimberly Johnson

"How do you capture a "REVOLTION?""
"How do you know when 1 is coming down the TRACK?"
"How will I know it's here? - cuz in HERE..it's awfully BLACK!!"
"Will I hear a whistle blowing? - Will it b visible - 4 the NAKED eye to
    C?"
"Is this REAL?" - I ask MYSELF - "Is the REVOLUTION..really meant
    for ME"

"Will it come up from the UnderGround darkness..like a thief in the
    NIGHT?"
Open the doors to a "PEACE TRAIN" - .and take me smoothly into the
    LIGHT?
I sat daily..waiting for my next obvious CLUE -
Then one day I FOUND IT - it came quietly - directly from "YOU"

YOUTUBE - lead me directly to it - all tracks led to a DR. RON PAUL -
That was IT - I'd found my TICKET - and on the sign read -   "PEACE
    TRAIN FOR ALL"
I would NEVER have guessed - This is what was to be effortlessly - .
    found
but I could hear the trains WHISTLE - It was visible - THE
    REVOLUTION was most definitely "OVERGROUND" -

I knew what to wear - I knew right where to stand..
So many beautiful people - open and willing to lend - A beautiful
    HELPING HAND.
I get up now everyday - knowing I'm not ALONE on this TRAIN
Now I can feel the "LOVE" - not the MATRIX - and it's PAIN..
Everyday - I can feel a change - IT'S the trains momentum GROWING..
I can't explain it..it's just a feeling..a true sense of KNOWING.

Singing songs of FREEDOM - for ALL the world to HEAR.
Just put your ear to the track my friends - the 'PEACE TRAIN" it's always
    NEAR.
You can step on any time you want - Your TICKET - is open-ended and
    FREE..
I'll reserve you a seat - I know a few people - U can sit right next to ME - .

I look forward to meeting YOU - and SO do my FRIENDS -
This really is a FREEDOM SONG - and FREEDOM never ENDS!

"OF ALL TYRANNIES,
A TYRANNY EXERCISED FOR THE
GOOD OF ITS VICTIMS MAY BE
THE MOST OPPRESSIVE."

C.S. LEWIS

"THERE IS NO FREEDOM WITHOUT COURAGE."

ERIC SCHAUB

Anarchism and American Traditions

by: Voltairine de Cleyre

American traditions, begotten of religious rebellion, small self-sustaining communities, isolated conditions, and hard pioneer life, grew during the colonization period of one hundred and seventy years from the settling of Jamestown to the outburst of the Revolution. This was in fact the great constitution-making epoch, the period of charters guaranteeing more or less of liberty, the general tendency of which is well described by Wm. Penn in speaking of the charter for Pennsylvania: "I want to put it out of my power, or that of my successors, to do mischief."

The revolution is the sudden and unified consciousness of these traditions, their loud assertion, the blow dealt by their indomitable will against the counter force of tyranny, which has never entirely recovered from the blow, but which from then till now has gone on remolding and regrappling the instruments of governmental power, that the Revolution sought to shape and hold as defenses of liberty.

To the average American of today, the Revolution means the series of battles fought by the patriot army with the armies of England. The millions of school children who attend our public schools are taught to draw maps of the siege of Boston and the siege of Yorktown, to know the general plan of the several campaigns, to quote the number of prisoners of war surrendered with Burgoyne; they are required to remember the date when Washington crossed the Delaware on the ice; they are told to "Remember Paoli," to repeat "Molly Stark's a widow," to call General Wayne "Mad Anthony Wayne," and to execrate Benedict Arnold; they know that the Declaration of Independence was signed on the Fourth of July, 1776, and the Treaty of Paris in 1783; and then they think they have learned the Revolution--blessed be George Washington! They have no idea why it should have been called a "revolution" instead of the "English War," or any similar title: it's the name of it, that's all. And name-worship, both in child and man, has acquired such mastery of them, that the name "American Revolution" is held sacred, though it means to them nothing more than successful force, while the name "Revolution" applied to a further possibility, is a spectre detested and abhorred. In neither case have they any idea of the content of the word, save that of armed force. That has already happened, and long happened, which Jefferson foresaw when he wrote:

"The spirit of the times may alter, will alter. Our rulers will become corrupt, our people careless. A single zealot may become persecutor, and better men be his victims. It can never be too often repeated that the time for fixing every essential right, on a legal basis, is while our rulers are honest, ourselves united. From the conclusion of this war we shall be going down hill. It will not then be necessary to resort every moment to the people for support. They will be forgotten, therefore, and their rights disregarded. They will forget themselves in the sole faculty of making money, and will never think of uniting to effect a due respect for their rights. The shackles, therefore, which shall not be knocked off at the conclusion of this war, will be heavier and heavier, till our rights shall revive or expire in a convulsion."

To the men of that time, who voiced the spirit of that time, the battles that they fought were the least of the Revolution; they were the incidents of the hour, the things they met and faced as part of the game they were playing; but the stake they had in view, before, during, and after the war, the real Revolution, was a change in political institutions which should make of government not a thing apart, a superior power to stand over the people with a whip, but a serviceable agent, responsible, economical, and trustworthy (but never so much trusted as not to be continually watched), for the transaction of such business as was the common concern and to set the limits of the common concern at the line of where one man's liberty would encroach upon another's.

They thus took their starting point for deriving a minimum of government upon the same sociological ground that the modern Anarchist derives the no-government theory; viz., that equal liberty is the political ideal. The difference lies in the belief, on the one hand, that the closest approximation to equal liberty might be best secured by the rule of the majority in those matters involving united action of any kind (which rule of the majority they thought it possible to secure by a few simple arrangements for election), and, on the other hand, the belief that majority rule is both impossible and undesirable; that any government, no matter what its forms, will be manipulated by a very small minority, as the development of the States and United States governments has strikingly proved; that candidates will loudly profess allegiance to platforms before elections, which as officials in power they will openly disregard, to do as they please; and that even if the majority will could be imposed, it would also be subversive of equal liberty, which may be best secured by leaving to the voluntary association of those interested in the management of matters of common concern, without coercion of the uninterested or the opposed.

Among the fundamental likeness between the Revolutionary Republicans and the Anarchists is the recognition that the little must precede the great; that the local must be the basis of the general; that there can be a free federation only when there are free communities to federate; that the spirit of the latter is carried into the councils of the former, and a local tyranny may thus become an instrument for general enslavement. Convinced of the supreme importance of ridding the municipalities of the institutions of tyranny, the most strenuous advocates of independence, instead of spending their efforts mainly in the general Congress, devoted themselves to their home localities, endeavoring to work out of the minds of their neighbors and fellow-colonists the institutions of entailed property, of a State-Church, of a class-divided people, even the institution of African slavery itself. Though largely unsuccessful, it is to the measure of success they did achieve that we are indebted for such liberties as we do retain, and not to the general government. They tried to inculcate local initiative and independent action. The author of the Declaration of Independence, who in the fall of '76 declined a re-election to Congress in order to return to Virginia and do his work in his own local assembly, in arranging there for public education which he justly considered a matter of "common concern," said his advocacy of public schools was not with any "view to take its ordinary branches out of the hands of private enterprise, which manages so much better the concerns to which it is equal"; and in endeavoring to make clear the restrictions of the Constitution upon the functions of the general government, he likewise said:

> "Let the general government be reduced to foreign concerns only, and let our affairs be disentangled from those of all other nations, except as to commerce, which the merchants will manage for themselves, and the

general government may be reduced to a very simple organization, and a very inexpensive one; a few plain duties to be performed by a few servants."

This then was the American tradition, that private enterprise manages better all that to which it IS equal. Anarchism declares that private enterprise, whether individual or cooperative, is equal to all the undertakings of society. And it quotes the particular two instances, Education and Commerce, which the governments of the States and of the United States have undertaken to manage and regulate, as the very two which in operation have done more to destroy American freedom and equality, to warp and distort American tradition, to make of government a mighty engine of tyranny, than any other cause, save the unforeseen developments of Manufacture.

It was the intention of the Revolutionists to establish a system of common education, which should make the teaching of history one of its principal branches; not with the intent of burdening the memories of our youth with the dates of battles or the speeches of generals, nor to make the Boston Tea Party Indians the one sacrosanct mob in all history, to be revered but never on any account to be imitated, but with the intent that every American should know to what conditions the masses of people had been brought by the operation of certain institutions, by what means they had wrung out their liberties, and how those liberties had again and again been filched from them by the use of governmental force, fraud, and privilege. Not to breed security, laudation, complacent indolence, passive acquiescence in the acts of a government protected by the label "home-made," but to beget a wakeful jealousy, a never-ending watchfulness of rulers, a determination to squelch every attempt of those entrusted with power to encroach upon the sphere of individual action - this was the prime motive of the revolutionists in endeavoring to provide for common education.

"Confidence," said the revolutionists who adopted the Kentucky Resolutions, "is everywhere the parent of despotism; free government is founded in jealousy, not in confidence; it is jealousy, not confidence, which prescribes limited constitutions to bind down those whom we are obliged to trust with power; our Constitution has accordingly fixed the limits to which, and no further, our confidence may go... In questions of power, let no more be heard of confidence in man, but bind him down from mischief by the chains of the Constitution."

These resolutions were especially applied to the passage of the Alien laws by the monarchist party during John Adams' administration, and were an indignant call from the State of Kentucky to repudiate the right of the general government to assume undelegated powers, for said they, to accept these laws would be "to be bound by laws made, not with our. consent, but by others against our consent--that is, to surrender the form of government we have chosen, and to live under one deriving its powers from its own will, and not from our authority." Resolutions identical in spirit were also passed by Virginia, the following month; in those days the States still considered themselves supreme, the general government subordinate.

To inculcate this proud spirit of the supremacy of the people over their governors was to be the purpose of public education! Pick up today any common school history, and see how much of this spirit you will find therein. On the contrary, from cover to cover you will find nothing but the cheapest sort of patriotism, the inculcation of the most unquestioning acquiescence in the deeds of government, a lullaby of rest, security, confidence--the doctrine that the Law can do no wrong, a Te Deum in praise of the continuous encroachments of the powers of the general government upon the reserved rights of the States, shameless falsification of all acts of rebellion, to put the government in the right and the rebels in the wrong, pyrotechnic glorifications of union, power, and force, and a complete ignoring of the essential liberties to maintain which was the purpose of the revolutionists. The anti-Anarchist law of post-McKinley passage, a much worse law than the Alien and Sedition acts which roused the wrath of Kentucky and Virginia to the point of threatened rebellion, is exalted as a wise provision of our All-Seeing Father in Washington.

Such is the spirit of government-provided schools. Ask any child what he knows about Shays' rebellion, and he will answer, "Oh, some of the farmers couldn't pay their taxes, and Shays led a rebellion against the court-house at Worcester, so they could burn up the deeds; and when Washington heard of it he sent over an army quick and taught 'em a good lesson"-"And what was the result of it?" "The result? Why--why--the result was--Oh yes, I remember--the result was they saw the need of a strong federal government to collect the taxes and pay the debts." Ask if he knows what was said on the other side of the story, ask if he knows that the men who had given their goods and their health and their strength for the freeing of the country now found themselves cast into prison for debt, sick, disabled, and poor, facing a new tyranny for the old; that their demand was that the land should become the free communal possession of those who wished to work it, not subject to tribute, and the child will answer "No." Ask him if he ever read Jefferson's letter to Madison about it, in which he says:

"Societies exist under three forms, sufficiently distinguishable. 1. Without government, as among our Indians. 2. Under government wherein the will of every one has a just influence; as is the case in England in a slight degree, and in our States in a great one. 3. Under government of force, as is the case in all other monarchies, and in most of the other republics. To have an idea of the curse of existence in these last, they must be seen. It is a government of wolves over sheep. It is a problem not clear in my mind that the first condition is not the best. But I believe it to be inconsistent with any great degree of population. The second state has a great deal of good in it...It has its evils too, the principal of which is the turbulence to which it is subject. ...But even this evil is productive of good. It prevents the degeneracy of government, and nourishes a general attention to public affairs. I hold that a little rebellion now and then is a good thing."

Or to another correspondent:

"God forbid that we should ever be twenty years without such a rebellion!...What country can preserve its liberties if its rulers are not warned from time to time that the people preserve the spirit of resistance? Let them take up arms... The tree of liberty must be refreshed from time to time with the blood of patriots and tyrants. It is its natural manure."

Ask any school child if he was ever taught that the author of the Declaration of Independence, one of the great founders of the common school, said these things, and he will look at you with open mouth and unbelieving eyes. Ask him if he ever heard that the man who sounded the bugle note in the darkest hour of the Crisis, who roused the courage of the soldiers when Washington saw only mutiny and despair ahead, ask him if he knows that this man also wrote, "Government at best is a necessary evil, at worst an intolerable one," and if he is a little better informed than the average he will answer, "Oh well, he [Tom Paine] was an infidel!" Catechize him about the merits of the Constitution which he has learned to repeat like a poll-parrot, and you will find his chief conception is not of the powers withheld from Congress, but of the powers granted.

Such are the fruits of government schools. We, the Anarchists, point to them and say: If the believers in liberty wish the principles of liberty taught, let them never entrust that instruction to any government; for the nature of government is to become a thing apart, an institution existing for its own sake, preying upon the people, and teaching whatever will tend to keep it secure in its seat. As the fathers said of the governments of Europe, so say we of this government also after a century and a quarter of independence: "The blood of the people has become its inheritance, and those who fatten on it will not relinquish it easily."

Public education, having to do with the intellect and spirit of a people, is probably the most subtle and far-reaching engine for molding the course of a nation; but commerce, dealing as it does with material things and producing immediate effects, was the force that bore down soonest upon the paper barriers of constitutional restriction, and shaped the government to its requirements. Here, indeed, we arrive at the point where we, looking over the hundred and twenty five years of independence, can see that the simple government conceived by the revolutionary republicans was a foredoomed failure. It was so because of: 1) the essence of government itself; 2) the essence of human nature; 3) the essence of Commerce and Manufacture.

Of the essence of government, I ha\re already said, it is a thing apart, developing its own interests at the expense of what opposes it; all attempts to make it anything else fail. In this Anarchists agree with the traditional enemies of the Revolution, the monarchists, federalists, strong government believers, the Roosevelts of today, the Jays, Marshalls, and Hamiltons of then--that Hamilton, who, as Secretary of the Treasury, devised a financial system of which we are the unlucky heritors, and whose objects were twofold: To puzzle the people and make public finance obscure to those that paid for it; to serve as a machine for corrupting the legislatures; "for he avowed the opinion that man could be governed by two motives only, force or interest"; force being then out of the question, he laid hold of interest, the greed of the legislators, to set going an association of persons having an entirely separate welfare from the welfare of their electors, bound together by mutual corruption and mutual desire for plunder. The Anarchist agrees that Hamilton was logical, and understood the core of government; the difference is, that while strong govermnentalists believe this is necessary and desirable, we choose the opposite conclusion, No Government Whatsoever.

As to the essence of human nature, what our national experience has made plain is this, that to remain in a continually exalted moral condition is not human nature. That has happened which was prophesied: we have gone down hill from the Revolution until now; we are absorbed in "mere money-getting." The desire for material east long ago vanquished the spirit of '76. What was that spirit? The spirit that animated the people of Virginia, of the Carolinas, of Massachusetts, of New York, when they refused to import goods from England; when they preferred (and stood by it) to wear coarse, homespun cloth, to drink the brew of their own growths, to fit their appetites to the home supply, rather than submit to the taxation of the imperial ministry. Even within the lifetime of the revolutionists, the spirit decayed. The love of material ease has been, in the mass of men and permanently speaking, always greater than the love of liberty. Nine hundred and ninety nine women out of a thousand are more interested in the cut of a dress than in the independence of their sex; nine hundred and ninety nine men out of a thousand are more interested in drinking a glass of beer than in questioning the tax that is laid on it; how many children are not willing to trade the liberty to play for the promise of a new cap or a new dress? That it is which begets the complicated mechanism of society; that it is which, by multiplying the concerns of government, multiplies the strength of government and the corresponding weakness of the people; this it is which begets indifference to public concern, thus making the corruption of government easy.

As to the essence of Commerce and Manufacture, it is this: to establish bonds between every corner of the earths surface and every other corner, to multiply the needs of mankind, and the desire for material possession and enjoyment.

The American tradition was the isolation of the States as far as possible. Said they: We have won our liberties by hard sacrifice and struggle unto death. We wish now to be let alone and to let others alone, that our principles may have time for trial; that we may become accustomed to the exercise of our rights; that we may be kept free from the contaminating influence of European gauds, pageants, distinctions. So richly did they esteem the absence of these that they could in all fervor write: "We shall see multiplied instances of Europeans coming to America, but no man living will ever seen an instance of an American removing to settle in Europe, and continuing there." Alas! In less than a hundred years the highest aim of a "Daughter of the Revolution" was, and is, to buy a castle, a title, and rotten lord, with the money wrung from American servitude! And the commercial interests of America are seeking a world empire!

In the earlier days of the revolt and subsequent independence, it appeared that the "manifest destiny" of America was to be an agricultural people, exchanging food stuffs and raw materials for manufactured articles. And in those days it was written: "We shall be virtuous as long as agriculture is our principal object, which will be the case as long as there remain vacant lands in any part of America. When we get piled upon one another in large cities, as in Europe, we shall become corrupt as in Europe, and go to eating one another as they do there." Which we are doing, because of the inevitable development of Commerce and Manufacture, and the concomitant development of strong government. And the parallel prophecy is likewise fulfilled: "If ever this vast country is brought under a single government, it will be one of the most extensive corruption, indifferent and incapable of a wholesome care over so wide a spread of surface." There is not upon the face of the earth today a government so utterly and shamelessly corrupt as that of the United States of America. There are others more cruel, more tyrannical, more devastating; there is none so utterly venal.

And yet even in the very days of the prophets, even with their own consent, the first concession to this later tyranny was made. It was made when the Constitution was made; and the Constitution was made chiefly because of the demands of Commerce. Thus it was at the outset a merchant's machine, which the other interests of the country, the land and labor interests, even then foreboded would destroy their liberties. In vain their jealousy of its central power made enact the first twelve amendments. In vain they endeavored to set bounds over which the federal power dare not trench. In vain they enacted into general law the freedom of speech, of the press, of assemblage and petition. All of these things we see ridden roughshod upon every day, and have so seen with more or less intermission since the beginning of the nineteenth century. At this day, every police lieutenant considers himself, and rightly so, as more powerful than the General Law of the Union; and that one who told Robert Hunter that he held in his fist something stronger than the Constitution, was perfectly correct. The right of assemblage is an American tradition which has gone out of fashion; the police club is now the mode. And it is so in virtue of the people's indifference to liberty, and the steady progress of constitutional interpretation towards the substance of imperial government.

It is an American tradition that a standing army is a standing menace to liberty; in Jefferson's presidency the army was reduced to 3,000 men. It is American tradition that we keep out of the affairs of other nations. It is American practice that we meddle with the affairs of everybody else from the West to the East Indies, from Russia to Japan; and to do it we have a standing army of 83,251 men.

It is American tradition that the financial affairs of a nation should be transacted on the same principles of simple honesty that an individual conducts his own business; viz., that debt is a bad thing, and a man's first surplus earning should be applied to his debts; that offices and office holders should be few. It is American practice that the general government should always have millions [of dollars] of debt, even if a panic or a war has to be forced to prevent its being paid off; and as to the application of its income office holders come first. And within the last administration it is reported that 99,000 offices have been created at an annual expense of 1663,000,000. Shades of Jefferson! "How are vacancies to be obtained? Those by deaths are few; by resignation none." Roosevelt cuts the knot by making 99,000 new ones! And few will die - and none resign. They will beget sons and daughters, and Taft will have to create 99,000 more! Verily a simple and a serviceable thing is our general government.

It is American tradition that the Judiciary shall act as a check upon the impetuosity of Legislatures, should these attempt to pass the bounds of constitutional limitation. It is American practice that the Judiciary justifies every law which trenches on the liberties of the people and nullifies every act of the Legislature by which the people seek to regain some measure of their freedom. Again, in the words of Jefferson: "The Constitution is a mere thing of wax in the hands of the Judiciary, which they may twist and shape in any form they please." Truly, if the men who fought the good

126

fight for the triumph of simple, honest, free life in that day, were now to look upon the scene of their labors, they would cry out together with him who said:

"I regret that I am now to die in the belief that the useless sacrifices of themselves by the generation of '76 to acquire self-government and happiness to their country, is to be thrown away by the unwise and unworthy passions of their sons, and that my only consolation is to be that I shall not live to see it."

And now, what has Anarchism to say to all this, this bankruptcy of republicanism, this modern empire that has grown up on the ruins of our early freedom? We say this, that the sin our fathers sinned was that they did not trust liberty wholly. They thought it possible to compromise between liberty and government, believing the latter to be "a necessary evil," and the moment the compromise was made, the whole misbegotten monster of our present tyranny began to grow. Instruments which are set up to safeguard rights become the very whip with which the free are struck.

Anarchism says, Make no laws whatever concerning speech, and speech will be free; so soon as you make a declaration on paper that speech shall be free, you will have a hundred lawyers proving that "freedom does not mean abuse, nor liberty license"; and they will define and define freedom out of existence. Let the guarantee of free speech be in every man's determination to use it, and we shall have no need of paper declarations. On the other hand, so long as the people do not care to exercise their freedom, those who wish to tyrannize will do so; for tyrants are active and ardent, and will devote themselves in the name of any number of gods, religious and otherwise, to put shackles upon sleeping men.

The problem then becomes, Is it possible to stir men from their indifference? We have said that the spirit of liberty was nurtured by colonial life; that the elements of colonial life were the desire for sectarian independence, and the jealous watchfulness incident thereto; the isolation of pioneer communities which threw each individual strongly on his own resources, and thus developed all-around men, yet at the same time made very strong such social bonds as did exist; and, lastly, the comparative simplicity of small communities.

All this has disappeared. As to sectarianism, it is only by dint of an occasional idiotic persecution that a sect becomes interesting; in the absence of this, outlandish sects play the fool's role, are anything but heroic, and have little to do with either the name or the substance of liberty. The old colonial religious parties have gradually become the "pillars of society," their animosities have died out, their offensive peculiarities have been effaced, they are as like one another as beans in a pod, they build churches - and sleep in them.

As to our communities, they are hopelessly and helplessly interdependent, as we ourselves are, save that continuously diminishing proportion engaged in all around farming; and even these are slaves to mortgages. For our cities, probably there is not one that is provisioned to last a week, and certainly there is none which would not be bankrupt with despair at the proposition that it produce its own food. In response to this condition and its correlative political tyranny, Anarchism affirms the economy of self-sustenance, the disintegration of the great communities, the use of the earth.

I am not ready to say that I see clearly that this will take place; but I see clearly that this must take place if ever again men are to be free. I am so well satisfied that the mass of mankind prefer material possessions to liberty, that I have no hope that they will ever, by means of intellectual or moral stirrings merely, throw off the yoke of oppression fastened on them by the present economic system, to institute free societies. My only hope is in the blind development of the economic system and political oppression itself. The great characteristic looming factor in this gigantic power is Manufacture. The tendency of each nation is to become more and more a manufacturing one, an exporter of fabrics, not an importer. If this tendency follows its own logic, it must eventually circle round to each community producing for itself. What then will become of the surplus product when the manufacturer shall have no foreign market? Why, then mankind must face the dilemma of sitting down and dying'inthe midst of it, or confiscating the goods.

Indeed, we are partially facing this problem even now; and-so far we are sitting down and dying. I opine, however, that men will not do it forever, and when once by an act of general expropriation they have overcome the reverence and fear of property, and their awe of government, they may waken to the consciousness that things are to be used, and therefore men are greater than things. This may rouse the spirit of liberty.

If, on the other hand, the tendency of invention to simplify, enabling the advantages of machinery to be combined with smaller aggregations of workers, shall also follow its own logic, the great manufacturing plants will break up, population will go after the fragments, and there will be seen not indeed the hard, self-sustaining, isolated pioneer communities of early America, but thousands of small communities stretching along the lines of transportation, each producing very largely for its own needs, able to rely upon itself, and therefore able to be independent. For the same rule holds good for societies as for individuals--those may be free who are able to make their own living.

In regard to the breaking up of that vilest creation of tyranny, the standing army and navy, it is clear that so long as men desire to fight, they will have armed force in one form or another. Our fathers thought they had guarded against a standing army by providing for the voluntary militia. In our day we have lived to see this militia declared part of the regular military force of the United States, and subject to the same demands as the regulars. Within another generation we shall probably see its members in the regular pay of the general government. Since any embodiment of the fighting spirit, any military organization, inevitably follows the same line of centralization, the logic of Anarchism is that the least objectionable form of armed force is that which springs up voluntarily, like the minute men of Massachusetts, and disbands as soon as the occasion which called it into existence is past: that the really desirable thing is that all men--not Americans only--should be at peace; and that to reach this, all peaceful persons should withdraw their support from the army, and require that all who make war shall do so at their own cost and risk; that neither pay nor pensions are to be provided for those who choose to make man-killing a trade.

As to the American tradition of non-meddling, Anarchism asks that it be carried down to the individual himself. It demands no jealous barrier of isolation; it knows that such isolation is undesirable and impossible; but it teaches that by all men's strictly minding their own business, a fluid society, freely adapting itself to mutual needs, wherein all the world shall belong to all men, as much as each has need or desire, will result.

And when Modern Revolution has thus been carried to the heart of the whole world--if it ever shall be, as I hope it will--then may we hope to see a resurrection of that proud spirit of our fathers which put the simple dignity of Man above the gauds of wealth and class, and held that to, be an American was greater than to be a king.

In that day there shall be neither kings nor Americans - only Men ; over the whole earth, MEN.

"LIBERTY IS LOST THROUGH COMPLACENCY
AND A SUBSERVIENT MINDSET."

RON PAUL

"THOSE WHO WOULD GIVE UP ESSENTIAL LIBERTY,
TO PURCHASE A LITTLE TEMPORARY SAFETY,
DESERVE NEITHER LIBERTY NOR SAFETY."

BENJAMIN FRANKLIN

USA, R.I.P.

October 29, 2001
by: Jim Davidson

Born in liberty 19 April 1775; Died 9 July 1868

A recent issue of The Libertarian Enterprise included the following dateline: "October 22, 2001 ... I Hear America Dying."

Sorry, guys. That isn't the sound of America dying. That's decompositional gas built up in the lungs, being released as one jackbooted thug after another treads on the body.

America as a concept of free people living in harmony is alive and well. As a constitutionally limited republic suitable for governing a free people, the USA is dead. It is now suffering the indignities of the descendants of the maniacs who killed it.

In recognizing the significance of the United States, it is appropriate to find words for the tombstone. I'd like to put forward an argument for birth date and death date. During the course of this argument, the body of this essay will constitute an obituary, which should help in the grieving process. At the end, a brief epitaph.

Born in Liberty

The birth of the USA as a country has as much to do with events on 19 April 1775 as it does with any other time. On that date, in battles at Lexington and Concord, the Sons of Liberty and their friends opposed with deadly force the attempt by British troops to seize their weapons. A few months later, the Continental Congress declared the independence which was already the subject of open warfare. In 1781, the British forces under Cornwallis, cut off on land by French, US and militia troops, and cut off on the sea by French and US navy vessels, surrendered. The date of 19 October 1781, when Cornwallis accepted terms and surrendered, is less meritorious, since additional battles at sea took place for some time thereafter. The Treaty of Paris in 1783 provided formal recognition of the new country.

The dark forces opposed to liberty saw within the nascent country a huge territory, a potentially powerful government, endless opportunities for wealth without working including special privileges and government contract fraud, and a certain tendency by an athletic minority to gung ho enthusiasm. They wanted to rule it, but to do so, its traditions of individual freedom had to be eviscerated.

They didn't take long to get started.

Shay Leads Revolutionary War Veterans

In 1786, in the beautiful Berkshires of Western Massachusetts, where I've spent many happy days, trouble was brewing. High taxes, high litigation fees, and unreasonable state legislation were driving farmers and tradesmen into poverty. The men who fought nobly and valiantly in the War of the Revolution were no longer content with their situation. Daniel Shays led them in armed insurrection. His revolt was brutally suppressed. However, it was a contributing factor in the demise of the Articles of Confederation, the first constitutional government of the USA.

In 1787, a new constitution was proposed. It gave the national government many powers avoided by the revolutionaries in framing the Articles of Confederation. There were national powers of taxation, eminent domain, and significant monetary power. With a bill of rights to secure all powers not granted to the federal government to the states or people, and to identify and guarantee important individual liberties, the new constitution was ratified over the warnings of patriots like Patrick Henry, who feared its consolidating features.

Congress Opens a Bank

Though this new constitution made no provision for a national bank, Congress acted to create one. The First Bank of the United States opened for business in 1791, with two million of its $10 million in capital subscribed by the USA federal government (paid in from customs duties collected). For amusement, the Bank then lent the USA government $2 million. Much of the rest of the funding of the bank was subscribed by foreign investors, especially in Britain.

Shortly thereafter, the Whiskey Rebellion was undertaken by more Western farmers, tired of paying high taxes. (Surely the abandonment of the Articles of Confederation, which promised a "perpetual union" but were in fact seceded from by all thirteen original states before they acceded to the new constitution, should have provided the strong central government necessary to prevent such rebellions? Apparently not.) That rebellion was also brutally suppressed.

The Warfare State

Wars with Native American Indians in the old northwest culminated in 1794 with a crushing defeat for the Indians at Fallen Timbers. Having gained from Virginia, Connecticut, Massachusetts and New York the cession of their lands in this region by 1787, the terms of expansion of the USA were established, much to the dismay of its former inhabitants. In 1795, the natives signed up to the Greenville treaty.

In 1798, USA warships engaged French warships in the Caribbean, following on the heels of the XYZ affair. Was it a war? Not if you go by the constitutional standard of a declaration of war, but the men in power didn't mind such details. The Alien Act, the Naturalization Act, the Alien Enemies Act, and the Sedition Act were also unconstitutional, but that didn't stop the regime running things. The undeclared war and the unconstitutional affronts to freedom led to the passage of the Virginia and Kentucky Resolutions, the first clear signs that all was not well with the new regime.

The Democratic Republicans assumed power in 1801, largely on their opposition to the conflict with France and these unconstitutional acts. The Naturalization Act was repealed, and others were allowed to expire.

That same year, Jefferson grew weary of payments for safe conduct in the Mediterranean, and the Tripolitan War was declared. It continued until 1805. Jefferson sent millions in gold to the dictator Napoleon for the Louisiana Territory, a thoroughly unconstitutional purchase over which he struggled considerably before going forward.

In 1811, repudiation of the features of the Greenville Treaty by the USA government led to more uprisings in the old northwest. Tecumseh and Shawnee Prophet were unsuccessful in their bid for a permanent country. Also that year, the First Bank expired. When its charter was not immediately renewed, Britain promptly invaded.

War with Britain

http://elsinore.cis.yale.edu/lawweb/avalon/statutes/1812-01.htm The war of 1812 raged for several years. Washington, DC was invaded by British troops, and they saw fit to criticize the architecture of the White House by burning it. Some reports indicate that papers relating to the ratification of the (original thirteenth) amendment punishing titles of nobility with political exile were sought by British officers and seized. (That amendment was properly ratified in 1819, but has since disappeared.)

The USA was finished with its war with Britain in 1815. So, it must have come as a relief when the nation of Algiers declared war, keeping hostilities for the warfare state toasty warm. When Stephen Decatur brought USA warships to Algiers, the bey quickly surrendered, so Decatur went on to force concessions from Tunisia and Tripoli in the next five weeks. (Why defeat one foreign power when you can defeat three?)

What to do with all that war materiel? In 1817, the opportunity arose to send a punitive expedition into Florida, then a Spanish territory, against the Seminole Indians who were tough tradesmen, happy to accept runaway slaves into their tribe, and pretty good at holding territory in the swamps. Andrew Jackson was happy to lead 3,000 troops for eleven months of fighting on foreign soil.

A Pattern Emerges

In 1800, E.I. DuPont had arrived in the United States. His land deal there failed, so he turned to his other talent -- learned from Lavoisier -- making gunpowder. His little factory on the Brandywine in Delaware was soon a major supplier to the USA military. Pressed by all kinds of debts, DuPont was quite happy about the large sales during the War of 1812. In 1822, he was appointed to the Second Bank of the United States as a director. His family would have significant influence on politics as the USA grew and prospered.

So, perhaps it is no wonder that an expedition to "pacify" Indians was mounted by Monroe's administration in 1819. This Yellowstone Expedition succeeded in causing the deaths of many USA soldiers, and not a few Indians. It was followed in 1823 by the Blackfeet Indian War, and a war with the Arikari. Plenty of gunpowder sales resulted.

This business of putting down Indian tribes, keeping the peace out West, and keeping on top of the fur trade was such good fun, that war was almost continuous from 1827 to 1896 with: the LeFevre Indian War of 1827; the Sac and Fox War of 1831; Black Hawk's War of 1832 (which included the massacre of men, women and children who had shown a white flag to the USA troops); Cherokee and Pawnee disturbances from 1833 to 1839; another Seminole Indian War, this time from 1833 to 1842 which included the tactic of wiping out privately held crops in Florida to starve the enemy into submission; wars with nations misidentified as Sioux, and with the Comanche and Navaho from 1848 to 1861; generalized Indian wars from 1865 to 1890; another war with the Lakota and Oglala called the Sioux Indian War from 1890 to 1891; and the Apache and Bannock Indian troubles of 1892 to 1896. In all, the West provided nearly continuous gun powder sales for government contractors for about three quarters of a century.

Having effectively destroyed all these other nations, the USA government interred the remains of their people in concentration camps, passed out blankets infected with smallpox, and quietly went about consolidating their gold-, oil-, and timber-rich lands out from under them.

But, I'm getting ahead of myself. And you're probably wondering: if the

USA as a nation dies in 1868, how come its government was still letting contracts in 1896? Good question. Bureaucracy, my friends, never dies. The individual bureau rat may die, or be exterminated, but the bureau goes on and on. Some think that the bureaucracy of the Roman Empire lives on today in the Roman Catholic Church. Certainly a number of invaders of China learned within scant generations that the Mandarin bureaucracy was undeniable.

Clearly, the interests of suppliers of materiel to the war machine were interested in as much consolidation of national authority and power as possible. They were not alone. They shared this interest with certain monied interests who sought to form a banking cartel.

Keep in mind that after the First Bank of the United States wasn't renewed, Britain invaded. The war to defend the USA against Britain (version 2) was very expensive. The difficulties of financing the war were used as a motivation for the creation of the Second Bank of the United States (the one on whose board of directors EI Du Pont got a seat). Now why should the Second Bank include a gunpowder maker as a director?

Well, Du Pont continued to have massive debts. Debt financing involved him in close ties with the banking community. The same was true of other Northern industrialists who were seeking to export their goods not only to other countries, but to the Southern states. Moving goods a long distance involved letters of credit, which would be paid off if the goods arrived in good order. Again, these debt instruments, as well as debt financing for factories, helped tie industrial interests with the banking community.

The unconstitutionality of the Second Bank came to a head with the Jackson veto of a bill to renew its charter in 1832. Jackson's veto message is not only a fine example of a constitutionality argument for veto, but also an excellent description of the problems of the banking cartel's control over economic matters. http://www.yale.edu/lawweb/avalon/presiden/veto/ajveto01.htm (Jackson's re-election in 1832 is noteworthy as the founding date of the Democratic Party, which was the effective heir of the Democratic Republicans.)

At the same time, Jackson had another worry. Tariff duties were a main funding source for the USA, and were mentioned in the constitution as a power of Congress. However, the 1828 and 1832 tariff acts were viewed by South Carolina, among other interests, as being improperly favorable to Northern industrial interests over Southern agricultural interests. Certainly, the tariffs raised some money for government, but they also effectively denied foreign suppliers access to the Southern market by making their goods uncompetitive. Retaliatory tariffs on USA exports hit the Southern producers hardest. Their agricultural exports weren't selling as well due to retaliatory tariffs, and they were paying much higher prices for imports, prices which the Northern industrialists only undercut by a small amount, pocketing the profits.

Tariff policy, in other words, operated as a way of collecting taxes disproportionately from Southerners, while subsidizing Northern industrial interests. Corporate welfare in the USA was born with three features: a tariff act beneficial to business, a national bank beneficial to selected banking interests, and, to be fair, the constitutional provisions for slavery (notably the return of fugitive slaves, a major financial burden on non-slave owners) which subsidized plantation owners in the South. These welfare provisions married nicely to the warfare state.

The Nullification Crisis

Jackson had vetoed the unconstitutional national bank, paving the way for a plethora of state banks, some of which gained benefit of federal deposits (and were called "pet banks" in the papers favoring the national bank). Private currency was issued by these banks, many of whom backed their paper with bullion or specie. The era of free banking would work very effectively until repudiated by the Federal Reserve Act in 1913. How would Jackson deal with the tariff issue?

This matter came to a head in the Nullification Crisis of 1832-1833. The concept of nullification by a state, as a party to the constitution, was propounded in 1799 by Jefferson and others in the Virginia and Kentucky Resolutions. Both the 1828 and 1832 tariffs were considered abominable by South Carolina's state legislators, so they called a convention. The convention nullified the tariffs, and South Carolina prevented their collection at South Carolina's ports.

In response, Jackson proposed and Congress passed the http://elsinore.cis.yale.edu/lawweb/avalon/presiden/proclamations/jack01.h tm Force Act which authorized force to collect the tariff duties. In effect, Congress declared war on South Carolina. Before force could be used, Jackson encouraged moderates, led by Henry Clay, to formulate a compromise. A different tariff act was passed by Congress and signed by the President. In response, South Carolina rescinded its nullification of the previous tariffs, but went forward with the nullification of the Force Act. So, nothing was resolved, except that lower tariffs were in place for some time. The nullification of the Force Act was ignored.

The USA military deployed in 1833 to suppress the Cherokee and Pawnee disturbances. While those battles were raging, a new dictator in Mexico decided to consolidate his power. Santa Anna established measures which removed certain guarantees of liberty from the 1824 constitution of Mexico, notably trial by jury.

138

Another Nation Founded in Liberty

Previously, Mexico had encouraged settlers from the USA to come to the northern Mexican province of Coahuila y Tejas to settle. The intention was for these colonists to provide a buffer between the Comanche nation and the Mexican settlements further South. With the new dictator came grievances from the colonists, and they sent their leader, Stephen Austin, to Mexico City to complain. He was thrown in prison. By October 1835, the conflict was military. A massacre at the Alamo in March 1836 helped consolidate support for the newly declared independence of the Republic of Texas, which won a decisive victory at San Jacinto in April 1836. By 1839, Texas was recognized by the USA, Mexico, Holland, France, Russia, and Britain.

The new nation became a considerable consumer of revolvers and gunpowder from the USA. In other ways, it was patterned after Southern states. Shortly after the Seminole war ended in 1842, war with Britain (1844) over Oregon territory was averted by diplomacy, and Texas was unconstitutionally annexed.

Seminoles to Oklahoma

The Seminole war of 1835 to 1842 provided a special insight into Andrew Jackson's mindset. The same president who had vetoed the Second Bank on constitutional grounds was presented with a decision by the USA Supreme Court regarding treaties which protected the Seminole Indians from aggression and displacement by the USA. Jackson's reply was that the Chief Justice had rendered his opinion, "now let him enforce it." Meanwhile, Jackson sent the USA army into Florida to evict the Seminoles.

The annexation of Texas occupies the thoughts of many http://www.texassovereignty.org/hist/index.html liberty-minded individuals in this country. However, the best that can be said about it was that it was an action in which the majority of the people of Texas consented. The ordinance of annexation was put before the people of Texas in a popular election, and was approved. It is noteworthy that the admissions of Louisiana (c. 1811) and Texas as states prompted secession movements in Northern states such as Massachusetts.

A War with Mexico

Mexico, however, felt it was unsatisfactory, and war was declared. By 1848, the invasion and conquest of Mexico was complete, and the settlement treaty obtained considerable Western territory, including

California, for the United States. This territorial expansion brought the United States into contact with Mormon settlements in Utah, which would subsequently be organized as a territory of the USA.

The expansion of territory following the victory over Mexico renewed concerns about the distribution of power between slave states and free states. Northern population had swelled the representation in the House of Representatives from that region, so the Senate's balance between the two sections was important to Southern interests. The two issues which focused that interest were tariffs and the fugitive slave issue; one a corporate subsidy for the north, the other a subsidy to Southern plantations.

Balance had been upset in 1818 with the prospective admission of Missouri. Though populated by slaveholders, the bill to admit Missouri was amended by a New York representative to require anti-slavery provisions in its constitution. A year later, Alabama entered as a slave state, bringing the number of slave states to parity with free states. In 1820, Maine was to be admitted as a free state, and the Missouri Compromise brought Missouri in as a slave state, to retain parity, but with the proviso that the territories north of Missouri's Southern boundary (36 degrees 30 minutes north latitude) should be brought in as free states.

California gained population rapidly after the discovery of gold there. In 1849, its territorial legislature applied for statehood as a free state. President Taylor was also encouraging New Mexico territory to consider entry as a free state. Southerners John C. Calhoun and Jefferson Davis opposed these ideas. The Compromise of 1850 carved an enormous amount of territory off of the state of Texas, initiated the concept of popular sovereignty to let the people of a territory choose whether to enter as a free state or slave state, organized Utah and New Mexico territories, paid $10 million against the debt of the Republic of Texas (still the responsibility of the Texas state government), outlawed the slave trade in the District of Columbia (though not the ownership of slaves), set up strict fugitive slave laws, and brought California in as a free state. Daniel Webster spoke eloquently in favor of these measures, and President Taylor's death and replacement by conservative Millard Fillmore helped the passage.

Final Solution?

This compromise was hailed as a final solution to the issues creating sectional differences. In celebration, further Indian wars were prosecuted against the Comanche and Navaho. (New Mexico territory was also territory of the Navaho nation.) Not even the publication of Uncle Tom's Cabin by Harriet Beecher Stowe, a work heavily influenced by the recently translated Communist Manifesto could spoil the high spirits.

A mere four years later, though, the Compromise of 1850 was specifically repealed in the passage of the Kansas Nebraska Act of 1854. To the surprise of no one, the previous boundaries of Texas were not restored. However, the concept of popular sovereignty, or as it was also called "squatter sovereignty" was maintained. Kansas and Nebraska were organized as separate territories, with the expectation from Southerners that Kansas would enter as a slave state and Nebraska as a free state. The matter was further focused on the debates then raging about the route for another business subsidy, the transcontinental railroad.

The Kansas-Nebraska act's passage was the trigger for the formation of a largely abolitionist political party, the Republicans. Their candidate, John C. Fremont, and the Whig/Know-Nothing candidate Fillmore would lose the 1856 presidential election to James Buchanan.

Bleeding Kansas, where I grew up, was the destination for all kinds of settlers from both North and South, with the intention of winning the popular election. In 1858, a state constitution favoring slavery was passed, and sent to Congress. President Buchanan recommended it be approved. Congress, however, rejected it. A second constitution, forbidding slavery, was passed in 1859. Kansas was admitted as a free state in 1861, well after its admission had prompted the Secession Crisis.

Buchanan's Key Four Years

Buchanan played an important role in many events leading up to the Secession Crisis. He was responsible in part for the Ostend Manifesto (prompted by the seizure by Spain of a US flag vessel which docked in Havana), which proposed that Spain sell the island to the USA, or it would be taken by force. That document created a furor among the abolitionists, and was repudiated by the USA State Department. So, war with Spain was averted temporarily, and making of Cuba a slave state was obviated. Unfortunately, lack of success in this endeavor focused more of the sectional controversy on Kansas.

Things in Utah weren't made more stable by Buchanan's decision to replace Brigham Young as governor. So there was a brief war with the Mormons, called the Utah War. The war effectively began 15 September 1857 when Young declared martial law, and ended in June 1858 when USA troops entered Salt Lake City. Hostilities continued to simmer for several more years. Among the issues of concern to the liberty community was the USA government's opposition to the private practice of polygamy, which was endorsed by the Mormon church of the time. By this time, reading the Constitution had gone out of favor.

About the same time, the US Supreme Court was inflaming sectional controvery with the Dred Scott case. In Scott v Sanford (misspelled Sandford in many official reports), the Court ruled that negro slaves had no standing as citizens, that acts by the US Congress prohibiting slavery in the territories were unconstitutional and void, and, incidentally, that Scott remained a slave in spite of his residence in a free state and a free territory for a span of years. Curiously, the Supreme Court upholding the constitutional provisions on slavery and fugitive slave issues became a source of anti-constitution feelings within the abolitionist movement.

Buchanan was also president during the early phases of the transcontinental railroad issue. The fact that a for profit transcontinental railroad would subsequently be built (by James J. Hill), operating at a profit during its entire building period, and without any subsidies from state or national government, was not yet known. Buchanan was an opponent of a national program to build the railroad, saying that any such transportation project would become a huge waste of taxpayer money, and the source of endless pork barrel politics. His words were prescient: the NASA space shuttle program has exactly those features. So, it would be private companies that built the first transcontinental railroad, but with significant federal subsidies for every mile of track laid.

The Power of Secession

So, we come at last to the Secession Crisis which so weakened the USA that its subsequent death became almost certain. Secession as a concept dates back at least as far as 933 B.C. when northern Israel seceded from the Davidian kingdom. Arguably, the thirteen colonies which formed the USA did so by seceding from Britain. Thereafter, they seceded from the "perpetual union" of the Articles of Confederation, and acceded to the constitution.

The secession crisis, like the nullification crisis before it, was based on the idea that the several states which formed the united States of America were independent and sovereign parties to an agreement, the constitution for the united States, which assigned certain powers and limited sovereignty to the national government, but retained significant powers and autonomy for the several states.

Any reading of the Bill of Rights, article 10, which reserves to the states and the people all powers not delegated to the national government or prohibited by the constitution to the states, should settle this issue immediately. However, constitutional theories, many of which arose from traditions of the British conception of a constitution, were propounded by many, including President Buchanan who opposed secession.

The election of Abraham Lincoln of the Republican Party in November 1860, brought the crisis to a head. Although he campaigned on the basis that the president had no power to emancipate slaves or enslave free men, he would subsequently do both. The Republican party had been organized almost exclusively in the northern section, and wasn't very popular in the South or West. It platform was certainly more favorably received by abolitionists than by slavery supporters.

So, beginning in December 1860 with the secession of South Carolina, a total of thirteen conventions representing individual states would be formed, would vote on secession, and in some cases would put the measure to popular vote. Florida, Alabama, Mississippi, Georgia, and Louisiana followed in early 1861, with Texas hard on their heels. The Texas ordinance of secession was passed in convention, with one AH Davidson voting in favor. On 28 February 1861, the people of Texas voted (votes counted in early March) by over 75% in favor, to reverse their earlier decision embracing annexation. They voted to secede. In a subsequent conference in Montgomery, Alabama, the seven states agreed to form a Confederacy. (Former governor of Texas Sam Houston would berate this decision with the words, "Why leave one failed union to join another?")

Following the opening of hostilities in April 1861, with the firing on Fort Sumter to rid the new Confederacy of foreign forts in its territory, Col. Robert E. Lee was recalled from Texas to Washington and offerred command of the Union armies. Virginia and North Carolina were prompted by the hostilities to secede, and Lee chose to remain loyal to Virginia. Lincoln's blockade of Southern ports and call for state militia troops to fight against the seceding states prompted Arkansas and Tennessee to secede, as well. In subsequent months, Missouri and Kentucky would have governments on both sides of the dispute. A fourteenth state was formed briefly when General Sibley tried to reach the Pacific, and organized the Arizona Republic. His failure to protect his supply train led to his retreat after several impressive victories.

The story of the Confederacy, its cabinet including Protestants, a Catholic, and a Jew, its constitution mirroring that of the United States with provision for line item veto but few other changes, and its efforts to maintain the integrity of constitutionally limited government is a story better told by others. During its existence, it imported not a single slave; all slaves in Confederate or Union territory had been brought in by ships flying the USA flag. In fact, Confederate vessels enforced the prohibition of the slave trade by firing on USA flagged vessels carrying slaves, to the delight of the British crown. Attempts to gain British or French recognition failed, however. Ultimately, even the slaveholding Empire of Brazil would refuse to recognize the Confederacy.

The War for Southern Independence was officially known as the War of the Rebellion for many years. Recently, Congress adopted the name "War Between the States." It is often referred to in the South as the War of

Northern Aggression.

This war shed the blood of one million and twenty thousand men on the field of battle. It led to about an equal number of civilian casualties (both death and injury) and to enormous property destruction. The war started over the issue of secession, whether states party to the constitution could withdraw from the union. The crisis was deliberately precipitated by US Army troop movements and by the firing on Fort Sumter, as both sides wanted escalation. (Davis argued that without hostilities, Virginia would never secede, and without Virginia, the South couldn't succeed.)

The Land of Lincoln

Abraham Lincoln was a powerful individual. His call for militia in April 1861 and his decision to blockade Southern ports certainly catalyzed events already in crisis. When some northern states were tardy in meeting their troop quotas, Lincoln implemented conscription, leading to draft riots in Boston, New York, and Philadelphia.

Early victories by the Confederacy weren't pressed home, because the Davis Administration wanted to create the impression that the war was over principles and not an effort by the South to gain territory. In 1862, the strategy of Lee to take Washington was defeated by the loss of a copy of his detailed orders to the enemy. The Battle of Antietam was, at best, a draw, but as it led to Lee withdrawing Confederate forces, Lincoln declared victory. With that minor victory, Lincoln announced the Emancipation Proclamation, which ostensibly freed slaves in Confederate held territory, while maintaining the slave status of slaves in Northern territory.

About this time, Lincoln asked General Dodge to join him in Council Bluffs, Iowa. They both bought land there. Subsequently, Lincoln would propose the Pacific Railway Act which would be passed by Congress. Lincoln's and Dodge's properties would be directly across from Union Station at the Eastern Terminus set by Congress; later, the Union Pacific Railroad, happy with its headquarters in Omaha, would be forced to build a bridge across the Missouri to comply with the federal law (and enhance the Lincoln and Dodge properties further).

Lincoln would have other innovations. He brought consternation to the banking profession by issuing greenback currency backed by nothing. In contrast, Confederate currency was a promise to pay in silver two years after a treaty of peace with the USA.

A further noteworthy action by Lincoln, who began the tradition of ruling by decree, issuing Executive Order #1 (which over the years has been followed by some 13,000 others), was his whistleblower regulation. He faced the considerable difficulty of corruption in military contracting, which had grown to a considerable scale. So, he hit upon the notion of awarding a 10% bounty on corrupt contracts or other contract fraud to whistleblowers. He rapidly turned the USA into a nation of tattletales. (To nobody's surprise, this approach to policing federal corruption with individual initiative has been renounced by the Justice Department in recent years, which wants to do the job itself, and not pay out the bounties.)

The Doomed CSA

In July 1863, at two decisive battles, at Vicksburg and at Gettysburg, the fate of the South was sealed. It was divided by the Mississippi River which was entirely occupied by Union forces, and it was unable to prosecute a decisive victory in Northern territory.

But, doomed or not, the CSA fought on. Pierre Gustave Toutant Beauregard, who ordered the firing on Ft. Sumter to open the war, victorious at First Manassas and at Shiloh, was in charge of the defense of Charleston. He admitted to the lieutenant operating the experimental CSA submarines against the blockading Union fleet that the war could not be won by the South, but that perhaps a few more battles could be.

The defeat of the Confederacy became less certain as the Summer of 1864 rolled on. A significant peace movement was gaining popularity in the North. The Democratic Party made it a feature of their platform, although their candidate, George McClellan, a Union General, wasn't enthusiastic about it. Had the Confederacy been able to retain its remaining territory through the election, it might well have prompted the election of a peace candidate. Lincoln's Republican Party friends were waning in power, and he would be re-elected, on the strength of Sherman's September destruction of Atlanta, as a third party candidate.

In March 1865, attempting to retain its sovereignty while gracefully accepting defeat, the Confederate Congress and President agreed to free the slaves. However, Lee's defeat, the abandonment of Richmond, and the surrender of Lee's army at Appomatox effectively ended the war. As late as November 1865, Confederate warships on the high seas were still fighting. But the war ended in defeat for the Confederates.

Radical Reconstruction

Lincoln's assassination brought to power his hand-picked vice president, Andrew Johnson. Johnson was from Tennessee, and was military governor of that state during the war. He was also determined to restore the country. To do so, he was happy to pardon any Confederate who would swear an oath to the constitution for the United States. Defeated, often starving, and not opposed to the actual language of the constitution, most Confederates did so.

Johnson's pardons aroused the anger of radical Republicans who wanted to see the Southern states subjugated, not restored. His efforts to recognize the pacification of various Southern states and bring their delegations into Congress infuriated the Republicans whose political majority was greatly extended by the 1866 elections.

In 1867, the Republicans passed, over Johnson's veto, a "tenure of office" act which was intended to prevent him from removing Edwin Stanton, his secretary of war. Johnson was correct in suspecting Stanton of conspiring with Congress to his detriment. In March 1868, the House voted articles of impeachment. The Senate narrowly refused to convict.

Amendments Passed and Presented

In this post-war backdrop, several amendments to the constitution were proposed. It is noteworthy that the legislatures of all the Southern states ratified the fourteenth amendment which ended involuntary servitude, except for punishing criminals.

However, even the "carpetbaggers and scalawags" elected after the war to the legislature of Texas were reluctant to ratify the fifteenth amendment, which included the following language in its fourth section:

The validity of the public debt of the United States, authorized by law, including debts incurred for payment of pensions and bounties for services in suppressing insurrection or rebellion, shall not be questioned. But neither the United States nor any State shall assume or pay any debt or obligation incurred in aid of insurrection or rebellion against the United States, or any claim for the loss or emancipation of any slave; but all such debts, obligations, and claims shall be held illegal and void."

This passage confounded the hopes of many carpetbaggers who had bought up Southern bonds and currency at fire sale prices after the war, expecting it to be redeemed by the state legislatures. It also upset those who felt that the previously constitutionally embraced practice of slavery involved private ownership of property which was now being taken away without any compensation, in direct violation of the Fifth Article of the Bill of Rights.

Death of a Nation

However, these issues were minor in comparison to the overwhelming power of that first sentence. In July 1868, the ratification of this amendment was recognized by the Secretary of State of the United States, in spite of Northern states successfully overturning their previous ratification ordinances. The question of whether this amendment was properly ratified has been settled by the US Supreme Court, if one is to accept their authority in the matter. (Since the late 1890s, copies of the constitution have been published without the thirteenth amendment punishing the acceptance of a title of nobility with political exile. Accordingly, this amendment is known as the Fourteenth Amendment, and is popular for its "equal protection" provisions for US and state citizens outlined in its first section.)

With this amendment, the validity of the debt of the United States became unquestionable. While the consolidation of their power would wait for the second decade of the twentieth century, the banking cartel had won its greatest victory. The United States could not repudiate its debt. The members of the House and Senate, who were not to be questioned in any other place for their comments on the floor of those august chambers, could not question the validity of the public debt there, or anywhere.

The importance of this turning point has been lost on most individuals, historians and enthusiasts alike. By removing its power over its debt, the United States government had ceased to be the organizing force of a sovereign nation, and had become the enforcement arm of the banking cartel. Within the lifetime of survivors of the brutal war which crushed the Confederacy, the bankers would consolidate their power with the passage of the Federal Reserve Act and the equally dubious ratification of the "sixteenth" amendment authorizing an income tax (which no two states ratified in the same language). They would spend over a decade moving gold to the Bank of England, then stimulate a panic in 1929 to gain more private property from foreclosure.

This consolidation of power is significant, but it is not the defining moment of the death of a nation. Without removing the public debt from potential threats of annulment, negotiation, repudiation, default, or non-payment, the banking cartel could not have amassed the power necessary to force through the passage of the Federal Reserve Act and the ratification of the income tax amendment. As it was, both issues were narrowly won. Had the passengers of the RMS Titanic all survived their passage to New York, the outcome of these two pieces of legislation might have been very different.

The defining moment when the USA ceased to exist as a sovereign nation with power over its destiny was 9 July 1868, when the ratification of this amendment was accepted. Since that time, the power of the several states and of the people has been weakened, the power of the federal government has strengthened, and the limitations of the constitution have been breached.

Armies of Resistance

Sensing this problem, many throughout the USA were willing to resist. From 1868 to 1876, numerous bands of resistance fighters, many organized by former Confederate General Nathan Bedford Forrest, made war on the occupying armies, the banking cartel, and the railroads. Debtors conspired to collect cash for paying off their debts, summoning bankers out to their remote farms and homes for payment in full. Once the receipt was written out, the banker would leave, and be robbed of the cash by one of the roving bands. The collected cash would be returned to its various owners. In this way, foreclosure was averted by a great many individuals.

Eventually, a peace was negotiated. In 1876, Congress passed the Posse Commitatus Act, withdrawing troops from the several states, and providing that the USA military would not be deployed in the states without either the request of the affected state or states, or a declaration of national emergency or war. (Notably, this act was violated in 1993 at Mt. Carmel in February and again in April.) Forrest saw in the election victories for Democrats in 1872 the success of his resistance movement, and formally disbanded all units under his command.

How the Free Were Enslaved

The blood on the last battlefields was not yet dry when the organization of the new regime was begun. The US Secret Service was established in 1865 to guard against counterfeiting of US coins and currency. Its power to protect the president followed the 1901 assassination of McKinley. Its operation as a Praetorian Guard to take out unwanted presidents (JFK) and prospects (RFK) has yet to be fully recognized.

The Indian wars continued unabated through 1896, when there were hardly any Indians left. In 1898, the debt burden was expanded with a war with Spain, which gained Puerto Rico and the Philippines for the USA, and led to an independent Cuba with strong ties to the USA. Military occupation of Cuba continued through 1902, and the naval base at Guantanamo Bay was established in 1903. It has been a permanent foreign post ever since.

Also in 1898, the dowager empress of China, Tz'u Hsi, supported an armed resistance to the partition, foreign domination, and forced opium addiction of her country, the I Ho Ch'uan or "righteous, harmonious fists." The English called them "Boxers" and worried about them.

Hukbalahaps are a clan in the Philippines who aren't enthusiastic about being dominated by others. Their insurrection in 1899 led to four years of USA military intervention. Some say that the .45 automatic was designed to address the difficulty of gunning down Huks with any lesser weapon.

In 1900, the USA military was sent to oppose the Boxers in Peking.

148

They joined forces in a suprising show of harmony with British, French, Russian, German, and Japanese troops, to put down the uprising and compel payment of $333 million in indemnity. The commercial treaties with China were further amended, and the stationing of foreign troops was enshrined. China's debt was greatly increased, to the delight of bankers everywhere.

President McKinley was another significant one-term president. His annexation of Hawaii, declaration of war against Spain, and involvement of the USA in the Boxer rebellion were significant hallmarks of an administration controlled largely by the industrialist Marcus Hanna. He was re-elected in 1900, and kept to the gold standard preferences of the banking cartel. (His opponent in 1896 and 1900 was William Jennings Bryan, who wanted a return to the free minting of silver which had been an ante-bellum mainstay of the economy. Minting only gold coins limited severely the availability of money, which led to widespread depreciation and various panics.) His idea of commercial reciprocity among nations, a sort of free trade concept, was not well received. The day after he announced this view, he was shot and killed. An "anarchist" was convenient to hand and blamed for the killing. Hatred of anarchy, the solution to government, reached a fever pitch in 1920 with the infamous Palmer raids that rounded up 3,000 immigrants, confiscated guns, and led to very few convictions.

Meanwhile, McKinley, being dead, handed over the reins of state to the first of the Roosevelts, Teddy. TR was an enthusiast of intervention in Central America, and pushed the Panama Canal plan. He was also big on nationalist, socialist parks, and nationalized a great deal of territory for the purpose. Reading up on the contents of his sausage, he hit upon the idea of the Food and Drug Administration which has arguably been responsible for more deaths in the 20th Century than even the War/Defense Department.

All these post-death attacks on private property and individual liberty were difficult to avert. The power of the states had been stripped after the Secession crisis. The Supreme Court had ruled in Texas v. White (1868) that secession was unacceptable, ignoring the 10th Article of the Bill of Rights. Exercising powers short of secession was difficult for the states, so effective opposition to federal aggression or usurpation of power was essentially nil.

Revisiting the Warfare State

Not being very clever about its overseas empire, the USA was forced to pacify Cuba with a three year military expedition in 1906 to 1909. Supervising the election of pro-US politicos wasn't sufficient, so the USA military returned in 1912 to put down a rebellion by blacks who were concerned about discrimination.

Similarly, the USA sent troops to Nicaragua to support its favored ruler there in 1912. That intervention lasted until 1925, but troops were promptly sent back in 1926 until 1932.

An incident with US sailors in Tampico in 1914 led President Wilson to send troops to Vera Cruz for six months. That was followed by a punitive expedition into Mexico from March 1916 to February 1917.

The first Haiti expedition, in 1915 was followed by a second Haiti expedition in 1919 until 1920. On top of all these interventions, the warfare state had time for a Dominican expedition in 1916, and entered the European war in 1917.

Further interventions in China led up to the opening of the Second World War. The Empire of Japan attacked Pearl Harbor, bringing the USA into that war, and Hitler and Mussolini conveniently declared war (surprising even their Japanese allies) to support their Axis friends.

Following WW2, the USA military was involved in interventions or operations in Afghanistan, Albania, Australia, Azores, Bolivia, Bosnia-Herzegovina, Cambodia, Canada, Colombia, Croatia, Diego Garcia, Dominican Republic, El Salvador, Germany, Greece, Greenland, Grenada, Haiti, Iceland, Iran, Iraq, Japan, Korea, Kosovo, Kuwait, Laos, Lebanon, Libya, New Zealand, Nicaragua, People's Republic of China (e.g., spy plane emergency landing), Philippines, Serbia, Somalia, Spain, Taiwan (Republic of China), Union of Soviet Socialist Republics (e.g., U2 crash), United Kingdom, Vietnam, and Yugoslavia. By no means is this list complete. For fun, you might look up each of these countries at http://www.cia.gov/ in their World Fact Book to see how much external debt they have.

The power of the military industrial complex to compel the collection of taxes, even ones of dubious or absent constitutionality, to spend those funds on military (or NASA) contracts, to exclude smaller contract firms or absorb them, to send USA troops on missions to collect on the foreign debts of various countries, to establish USA foreign policy, to coerce and enforce, and ultimately to inspire terror, is a power which is married to the financial power of the banking cartel. Keeping the masses in line, the system of corporate welfare of the 19th Century was broadened into a system of individual welfare through direct payments and benefits in the 20th Century.

Zombie: The Living Dead

How has all this happened? One would have expected that the death knell of the USA would have ended its power. Instead, it has become a zombie, one of the living dead. In place of the constitutionally limited republic which was founded after the Revolutionary War, the USA government has been occupied by a legion of misfits, unwilling to work for a living, unskilled at anything but machination, and willing to see anyone killed for their success at gaining or keeping power.

This entity has used chemical, biological, and nuclear weapons against civilians in both war and peace. It has nuked Texas, Nevada, and Utah. Its reach even extended to the surface of the Moon, though not for economic purposes, but merely to defeat Soviet efforts in that direction. (It is noteworthy that the men who walked on the Moon all had significant military service; most were active military at the time.)

As a practical matter, therefore, opposition to this entity in the political realm of popular elections seems silly. It hasn't stopped at assassination, nor shown signs of squeamishness at the massacre of civilians. Burning seven dozen Texans in their church in 1993 was certainly not its worst crime against humanity.

On the world stage, the same individuals and influential companies are responsible for much that is wrong with the UN, the World Trade Organization, the World Bank, and the OECD nations in general. Watching these people make a mess of one country after another in the name of economic reform or austerity measures is a popular form of macabre humor.

Epitaph

You were promised an epitaph, and here it is:

The United States of America was conceived to secure the blessings of liberty to generations of Americans. It was hijacked by narrow economic interest groups, turned to evil, and obliterated as a sovereign power before its first centennial. Thereafter, its shell was turned to the conquest and destruction of other nations, the repatriation of foreign debts, and the subjugation of the American people. It stopped being about freedom a long time ago, yet the memory of its foundation by brave men as a home for the free lives on. Its Bill of Rights and the tradition of private property ownership in the USA established the basis for every freedom movement since. The first shot fired at the Battle of Lexington on 19 April 1775 was heard around the world through the effects of the freedom revolution. One day that revolution will return to American shores to finish its work. USA: the once and future free.

"LET ME BE A FREE MAN,
FREE TO TRAVEL, FREE TO STOP, FREE TO WORK,
FREE TO TRADE WHERE I CHOOSE,
FREE TO CHOOSE MY OWN TEACHERS,
FREE TO FOLLOW THE RELIGION OF MY FATHERS,
FREE TO TALK, THINK AND ACT FOR MYSELF --
AND I WILL OBEY EVERY LAW OR SUBMIT TO THE PENALTY."

CHIEF JOSPEH

My Allegiance

by: Jessica Pacholski

I pledge my allegiance to
FREEDOM.
To myself
to my family
my friends
my community.
To those who struggle and
to those who suffer needlessly.
I pledge my allegiance to the values
and morals of those who
founded this country.
To the men and women
who question authority;
who don't settle for
doing what they're told.
To those who seek the Truth
and follow the Natural Law

I pledge no allegiance to
ANY government.
I pledge no allegiance to
ANY politician.
I pledge no allegiance
to lies or uneducated whims.
I worship no man
nor will I sell my mind to
the highest bidder.
I will be no ones serf,
nor anyone's slave.

"FREEDOM LIES IN BEING BOLD."

ROBERT FROST

"Imprisoned" - by: Melody Key

"ONE OF THE PENALTIES FOR REFUSING
TO PARTICIPATE IN POLITICS
IS THAT YOU END UP BEING
GOVERNED BY YOUR INFERIORS."

PLATO

Reactivating the Liberty Movement

by: Allison Gibbs

Are we images of our previously selves? Mere reflections of seconds previously?

How do we decipher what is and what was? What exists and what doesn't?

I would argue that this physical realm means nothing. It is illusionary and once we become trapped within it- we lose our true selves. - The good we contain outside of these walls of perceptive reality.

Not exist- but to truly live?

Why do we allow ourselves to fall into this cyclical pattern and lose ourselves over and over again?

When will we see that once we let go- we will truly live?

Trapped in that Damned cave again. Alone- and we see ourselves as hopeless....

That is why I believe this movement is so important. And not the movement itself- but rather those that are pushing that movement- us.

We have to go back into that cave and pull out those of us that are still asleep. We have to awaken others up just as we have awoken.

And this will not be easy... wont be an overnight job.

And if we realize that all that we have been taught in this physical realm was an illusion- we can transcend.

When will we connect to one another and daily reactivate ourselves in what is important?

I refuse to go through the cycle again. and I refuse for the Liberty movement family to either. That is why I am here- to motivate and keep everyone in the fold- keep them steadfast in awakening others.

So, lets go out and make a difference. Lets Live rather than exist.

I appreciate what you are doing for both yourself and the movement.

"LIBERTY IS ALWAYS DANGEROUS,
BUT IT IS THE SAFEST THING WE HAVE."

HENRY EMERSON FOSDICK

ABOUT THE AUTHORS/ARTISTS

Adam Kokesh

Adam Kokesh was born on February 1st 1982 to a llama and an orangutan. This odd couple produced the predictably unpredictable offspring. Adam was also born with three nipples, but this has not been a hindrance to his moderately successful career as a circus sideshow accountant. He currently resides in a tree house and is hoping the kid who built it doesn't tell his parents.

Allison Gibbs

Allison Gibbs recently relocated to Washington D.C. from Atlanta via Charleston, South Carolina to work as the Director of Outreach for the Campaign for Liberty's national HQ. She previously worked as a microbiologist working on AIDS/HIV research and Antibiotic Resistance/Bio-Terror. Allison also aided in the South Carolina Primary and was the interim State Coordinator for the Rally for the Republic.

Bonita Honhorst

Bonita Honhorst is an Artist, Genealogist and a Grassroots Activist. Bonita has lived in San Antonio, Texas for 23 years. She began painting in acrylics in 2001, tried her hand at watercolor and pastels but focuses on oils currently. She was an Asst. Organizer for the Ron Paul San Antonio group, a Republican Precinct Chair and Delegate. In 2008, she was instrumental in opening a local office and organizing the delegates for Ron Paul to the Texas State GOP convention and the Republican National Convention. She is now working with The Texas Liberty Campaign and We Are Change San Antonio.

Brandon Trent

Brandon Trent was born in 1985 and currently resides in Danville VA. He works full time for Wal-Mart is single; and has no children.

ABOUT THE AUTHORS/ARTISTS

Danielle Kays

Danielle Kays is a wife and mother; an American whose lineage stretches back to Native Americans, English and Scottish settlers in the 17th century, and German settlers in the 18th century. She is a 6th-generation Texan whose family tree is full of farmers and statesmen, entrepreneurs and lawmen, explorers and pioneers, community founders and elected officials, risk-takers and military leaders. A Republican who is dismayed at how far the party has strayed from its conservative values; Danielle considers herself a quasi-writer with dozens of published articles in various small-time newsletters and a copy writer of website content, press releases, and other marketing and PR materials.

Darryl W. Perry

Darryl W. Perry is an Activist, Author, Comedian, Photographer, Philosopher, Poet & Statesman. He was born and raised in Birmingham, AL and the surrounding area. His first book 1776 & Today: Why We Need A New American Revolution was published in the spring of 2008 and was turned into a documentary. His second book, Grey is Not a Color was published in January 2009. Darryl has appeared on several internet broadcasts talking about his book and his political career and goals; which include being the 2004 Libertarian Party candidate for Pennsylvania State Treasurer; 2007 candidate for Mayor of Birmingham, Alabama; 2008 Alabama Statesmen/Boston Tea Party nominee/write-in candidate for US Senate and Darryl will be running for President in 2016.

Emma Goldman

Emma Goldman (June 27, 1869   May 14, 1940) was an anarchist known for her political activism, writing and speeches. She played a pivotal role in the development of anarchist political philosophy in North America and Europe in the first half of the twentieth century.

Goldman was well-known during her life, described as   among other things   "the most dangerous woman in America". After her death and through the middle part of the 20th century, her fame faded.

ABOUT THE AUTHORS/ARTISTS

Gary Chartier

Gary Chartier is Associate Professor of Law and Business Ethics at La Sierra University. He is the author of Economic Justice and Natural Law (Cambridge University Press 2009) and The Analogy of Love (Imprint Academic 2007), and of articles in journals including Legal Theory, Ratio Juris, and the Oxford Journal of Legal Studies. He holds a PhD from the University of Cambridge and a JD from UCLA.

Gary Franchi

Gary Franchi is founder of the Lone Lantern Society of America, a network of truth seekers that spans the globe working at the grassroots level to reach the people and empower them to act in the name of freedom, and has continued the legacy of Aaron Russo via Restore the Republic and Republic Magazine. Gary is a dedicated leader, researcher, video activist, writer and poet.

Henry David Thoreau

Henry David Thoreau (born David Henry Thoreau; July 12, 1817   May 6, 1862) was an American author, poet, naturalist, tax resister, development critic, surveyor, historian, philosopher, and leading transcendentalist. He is best known for his book Walden and his essay, Civil Disobedience. His philosophy of civil disobedience influenced the political thoughts and actions of such later figures as Leo Tolstoy, Mahatma Gandhi, and Martin Luther King, Jr. Thoreau is sometimes cited as an individualist anarchist as well as an inspiration to anarchists. Though Civil Disobedience calls for improving rather than abolishing government   "I ask for, not at once no government, but at once a better government"   the direction of this improvement aims at anarchism: " That government is best which governs not at all;   and when men are prepared for it, that will be the kind of government which they will have."

ABOUT THE AUTHORS/ARTISTS

James Russell Lowell

James Russell Lowell (February 22, 1819   August 12, 1891) was an American Romantic poet, critic, editor, and diplomat. He is associated with the Fireside Poets and believed that the poet played an important role as a prophet and critic of society.

Jessica Pacholski

Jessica Pacholski was born in 1973 and currently resides in North Carolina. She is full time mother of three and a part time writer and always a radical libertarian. She loves to paint and dance and is an exceptional cook when she feels like it. Everything she learned in her life she learned from living it and loving it. She credits Robert Heinlein with curing her of her flirtation with socialism when she was younger and Ron Paul with bringing her to the freedom movement.

Jim Davidson

Jim Davidson is an author and entrepreneur. He grew up in Kansas, was valedictory speaker for high school graduation, won sundry scholarships, got a BA in history at Columbia and an MBA at Rice. Past work included banking during college, aerospace during graduate school, a deal with the Soviet space agency to put an American on Mir, several new country ventures including travel on four continents, and many gold-related projects. His current venture is a film and online game project based on the book Alongside Night.

Kimberly Johnson

Kimberly Johnson currently lives in Sedona, Arizona and is the CEO and founder of BrightIris Productions. A background in Occult studies, acting, writing, producing, and broadcasting led her to her brain-child "Over-Ground RailRoad". Inspired by Ron Paul at every stop; her efforts continue to grow. A fan of Austrian Economics, her goal now is to build a new business paradigm and ride into the sunset on the "PEACE TRAIN". She is currently Producing "OverGround RailRoad" an Internet TV show. Topics of discussion include:Politics, Religion, Sex, Occult, & Spirituality

ABOUT THE AUTHORS/ARTISTS

Melissa Hill

Melissa Hill is a former Oregonian and current Minneapolis resident and grassroots activist. She holds three degrees including a Masters in Psychology. In the past, she helped organized the Minneapolis portion for the Great American Walk for Freedom, a group that walked from Green Bay to Minneapolis. After being mass-arrested and seeing the police state in full force during the RNC, she also works with the Community RNC Arrestee Support Structure (CRASS) as an advocate for the rights of the other 800+ arrestees. She also is currently involved in organizing the local rallies for End the Fed Minneapolis.

Melody L. (Lewis) Key

Melody Key was born in Grand Rapids , Michigan in 1971 and currently reside in East Meredith, NY with her husband Leon, two boys (Eric and AJ), and dog (Molly). For 35 years, she drifted in and out of life, only existing, never truly living . A little under 3 yrs ago, she experienced an epiphany of sorts.....her life started to change and grow in new and exciting directions. Melody realized life was meant to live, NOT to merely exist within the confines of societal dictates. She rediscovered herself and who She was through her spirituality and artistic interpretations.
Her goal is to continue portraying our world and it's beauty and/or ugliness for all to dissect or appreciate.

Patrick Henry

Patrick Henry (May 29, 1736   June 6, 1799) was a prominent figure in the American Revolution, known for his "Give me Liberty, or Give me Death!" speech. Along with Samuel Adams and Thomas Paine, he is remembered as one of the most influential (and radical) advocates of the American Revolution and republicanism, especially in his denunciations of corruption in government officials and his defense of historic rights.

ABOUT THE AUTHORS/ARTISTS

Richard Henry Lee

Richard Henry Lee (January 20, 1732 — June 19, 1794) was an American statesman from Virginia best known for the motion in the Second Continental Congress calling for the colonies' independence from Great Britain. His famous resolution of June 1776 led to the United States Declaration of Independence, which Lee signed. He also served a one-year term as the President of the Continental Congress, and was a U.S. Senator from Virginia from 1789 to 1792, serving during part of that time as one of the first Presidents pro tempore.

Terri Kurowski

Terri Kurowski is a cynical, freedom-loving, 50-something mother of 3 wonderful children, originally from Lexington, KY, now living in Norfolk, VA. She holds a BS in Agriculture from the University of Kentucky. Terri is a Certified Golf Course Superintendent (CGCS) who had a 20+ year career in golf course work. She now works as a Realtor and is considering other career opportunities. She loves to garden, read, write political opinion and debate politics. Her main goal in life is to help return our country to its limited form of government and to promote sound monetary policy and plans to run for office some day soon.

Thomas E. Woods, Jr.

Thomas E. Woods, Jr., is a senior fellow at the Ludwig von Mises Institute. He holds a bachelor s degree in history from Harvard and his master s, M.Phil., and Ph.D. from Columbia University. He has authored and edited over 1 dozen books, including multiple New York Times Bestsellers.

ABOUT THE AUTHORS/ARTISTS

Voltairine De Cleyre

Voltairine de Cleyre (November 17, 1866   June 20, 1912) was an American anarchist activist. During her time in the freethought movement in the mid- and late 1880s, de Cleyre was especially influenced by Thomas Paine, Mary Wollstonecraft, and Clarence Darrow. Other influences during her life were Henry David Thoreau, Big Bill Haywood, and later Eugene Debs. After the hanging of the Haymarket protesters in 1887, however, she became an anarchist. "Till then I believed in the essential justice of the American law of trial by jury," she wrote in an autobiographical essay, "After that I never could". Emma Goldman called her "most gifted and brilliant anarchist woman America ever produced"

FOR MORE INFORMATION

Freeople.com	Freedom + People = Freeople
LewRockwell.com	Lew Rockwell (anti-state, anti-war, pro-market)
Mises.org	Von Mises Institute
Antiwar.com	Anti-War
CampaingForLiberty.com	Campaign for Liberty
BostonTea.us	Boston Tea Party
LP.org	Libertarian Party
DownsizeDC.org	DownsizeDC
RestoretheRepublic.com	Restore The Republic
PositiveLiberty.com	Positive Liberty blog
BureauCrash.com	Bureaucrash
BreakTheMatrix.com	BTM Media
PeaceFreedomProsperity.com	Peace Freedom Prosperity
Theadvocates.org/links.html	Links from Advocates for Self-Gov't
Justin.tv/BoldSpeakTV	OVERGROUND RAILROAD
Kokesh.blogspot.com	Blog of Adam Kokesh
AllisonGibbs.com	Blog of Allison Gibbs
Liberalaw.blogspot.com	Blog of Gary Chartier
Nakedliberty.blogspot.com	Blog of Danielle Kays
Tertiumquids.blogspot.com	Blog of Terri Kurowski
TomWoods.com	Official site of Tom Woods
Indomitus.net	Official site of Jim Davidson
DWP2016.org	Official site of Darryl W. Perry 2016